"Pain is a natural part of human existence. But some wounds are so deep they impact how we live and who we are. Jimmy Evans shines a light on those dark, unhealthy places—all while pointing readers toward God, the source of true healing."

—**Dr. Tony Evans**, senior pastor, Oak Cliff Bible Fellowship; president, The Urban Alternative

"Jimmy Evans teaches us the power of surrender in his new book *When Life Hurts*. His biblical and honest approach will help free us from past hurts and struggles as well as serve as an important tool to help others who have experienced wounding from their past. A must-read for everyone!"

—**Joni Lamb**, cofounder, Daystar Television Network

"Life hurts and past wounds are sensitive topics. When I'm struggling with personal pain, I want to receive advice only from someone trustworthy who truly understands God's heart. I can't imagine anyone more trustworthy and more qualified than Jimmy to handle such a tender issue. *When Life Hurts* lovingly deals with all types of scarring experiences and speaks God's truth into each and every one. Read this book with an open heart and receive his healing."

—**Debbie Morris**, executive pastor, Gateway Church in Dallas/Fort Worth; bestselling author, *The Blessed Marriage* and *The Blessed Woman*

"There is so much pain in this world. All of us have been affected by it in some way. Whether it's loss, hurt, or rejection, the pain we experience is often unresolved. Jimmy Evans is a true father in the faith. He has written a powerful book that will bring you from a place of hurting to true healing in God."

—**Stovall Weems**, lead pastor, Celebration Church

"During our lifetime on this earth, every one of us will experience hurt, and sometimes we are hurt deeply. My husband, James, and I have felt this on occasions when people misunderstood our journey with Christ, the stands we have taken, and strong beliefs we hold. Never, however, have we encountered such anguish as with the recent passing of our youngest daughter, Robin. Our very close friend Jimmy Evans offers meaningful help to every one of us who has endured the indescribable pain of unexpected, deep hurt. In this book you will find help and healing for the deepest wounds in your heart. Thank you, Jimmy, for helping bind up broken hearts."

—**Betty Robison**, cohost, *LIFE Today*

"To a culture that says you can do and be anything if you set your mind to it, Jimmy Evans suggests a different path: that some hurts are impossible to escape by simply gritting your teeth and pressing on. Sometimes you need the healing hand of God. That hope is evident on every page of this book."

—**Christine Caine**, founder, The A21 Campaign; bestselling author, *Undaunted*

when
life
hurts

Finding *hope* and *healing* from
the pain you carry

JIMMY EVANS
with Frank Martin

BakerBooks
a division of Baker Publishing Group
Grand Rapids, Michigan

Published by Baker Books
a division of Baker Publishing Group
P.O. Box 6287, Grand Rapids, MI 49516-6287
www.bakerbooks.com

Printed in the United States of America

Library of Congress Cataloging-in-Publication Data is on file at the Library of Congress, Washington, DC.

ISBN 978-0-8010-1477-2

Published in association with the literary agency of Alive Communications, Inc., 7680 Goddard Street, Suite 200, Colorado Springs, CO 80920, www.alivecommunications.com.

To protect the privacy of those who have shared their stories with the author, some details and names have been changed.

13   14   15   16   17   18   19   7   6   5   4   3   2   1

To my precious wife, Karen. You have been my best friend and devoted partner for over forty years. You have been long-suffering and faithful in the good times and bad. You have walked the pathway of healing with me as God has used you more than any other person to help heal the hurts of my past and minister his love to me. This book would not be possible without you.

Contents

Contents

Foreword

As a frequent traveler, I'm always fascinated by what others take with them and how they carry it. So many people lug around these huge suitcases and duffle bags, enormous purses, and overstuffed backpacks. It not only slows them down but also makes travel more difficult, always dragging stuff from place to place. So I've learned to travel light, which is exactly what this book will help you do.

No one intends to carry around so much baggage, but it happens to everyone. Your life starts off innocently enough. As a child, you enjoy playing make-believe, chasing one another outside, and swinging on the playground. Even if you encounter a bully or not-so-nice teacher, you're still full of hope and idealism. You look forward to getting older and enjoying more of what's ahead of you.

But then life's path takes a detour and trouble starts interrupting your journey in ways you never saw coming. You face a devastating loss and suddenly things no longer look so simple and innocent. The world is no longer the place you thought it was. Life is not as fair as you had once hoped. You try to do the right things, but following the rules can't guarantee you the security you so desperately crave.

So you make some bad choices, the kind with repercussions that don't go away. Maybe it's a habit that leads to an addiction. Maybe it's hanging out with the wrong crowd or dating the wrong kind of person. Maybe it's cutting corners at work. Maybe it's settling for something that kills your dreams. Once you're angry and hurt, though, you figure you might as well try to find pleasure anywhere you can.

Then other people in your life start doing things and saying things that hurt even more. Some of these experiences come from family members who say things that cut to the heart and leave wounds that just won't go away. Others come from random people who seem intent on destroying your life. All of a sudden, you've got some baggage.

It's usually not much at first—you know, just the carry-on type that you can wheel behind you or wear on your back. You think you can manage it, so you learn to compensate and just accept how it weighs you down. Then more stuff happens. And before you know it, there's even more baggage.

And then you begin to think that this is just the way it will always be. You grow weary and ache from the burdens that seem to pile on you from every direction. With each step, your journey gets tougher, and you feel resigned to despair. Life weighs you down and crushes your spirit, and you become convinced that there's no way out.

Sound familiar?

Well, now is the time for you to finally be free from all of the pain and baggage. Aren't you ready to be free, to lighten your load and experience new joy and fresh peace? The answer is obviously "yes," but the real question is "how?"

For me, the most liberating moment of any trip occurs when I realize I have nothing to carry through the airport terminal. Not only did I pack light, but I also checked my bags. You can do the same as you read this book.

In the pages that follow, my friend and fellow pastor Jimmy Evans will help you lighten the load you've accumulated over a lifetime. With his help, you'll discover where your baggage came from and why you continue to carry so much of it around everywhere you go. More importantly, you'll understand how you can let it go and walk in the freedom of God's grace. Jesus said, "My yoke is easy and my burden is light" (Matt. 11:30). With biblical insight and practical wisdom, Jimmy will show you how to make this promise a reality.

Get ready. You're in store for a faith-filled journey of hope and healing.

Godspeed,
Chris Hodges
Bestselling author of *Fresh Air*

Acknowledgments

This project has been a joy because of the quality people I have been privileged to work with. I want to thank Baker Books for believing in me and making this book possible. Jon Wilcox, Michael Cook, Ruth Anderson, Anna Scianna, and the entire team at Baker Books are the best.

This is the second book I have written with my collaborator, Frank Martin. Frank is the best writer I've ever worked with. He helped me focus, organize, and maximize the message of this book in a way I couldn't have done without him.

Joel Kneedler and my friends at Alive Communications put me together with Frank and Baker Books. I will be forever grateful for their belief in me and their professional guidance.

Thanks also to my son, Brenton Evans, who is the president of MarriageToday and a marketing expert. Not only do I have the joy of working with my son—I get the constant benefit of his wisdom. I also want to thank Dan Millheim, Jana Shiewe, Shelly Millheim, and our entire MarriageToday team for their support and professional excellence.

Last and definitely not least, thank you to the elders, staff, and congregation of Trinity Fellowship Church in Amarillo, Texas, for their incredible love and support. Karen and I became members of Trinity in 1979. We were the walking wounded. At Trinity we found the most loving people we had ever met. All these years later, we haven't changed our minds. Thank you for believing and investing so much in us.

−1−

Pictures of Pain

There is a sacredness in tears. . . . They are messengers of overwhelming grief . . . and unspeakable love.

—*Washington Irving*

On a dresser in our home two framed photographs sit side by side—one of me, and one of Karen. We are both about ten years old, both smiling widely and sitting atop the same brown and white Shetland pony. You can tell it's the same horse in both photos by the unique markings on its mane.

Karen and I are both wearing chaps, and we both have on the same black cowboy hat and brown scarf. I've got on my favorite baseball shirt, and a big white bandage is wrapped around my left elbow. I had fallen the day before and gashed it. Karen is wearing a two-toned top and looks as cute as a bug with her cropped blonde hair and precious little smile.

They look like the kind of pictures you'd get if you went to a rich kid's birthday party, where the dad sprung for a clown and a caterer and about five hundred helium balloons, then rented a pony for the day so all the kids could have their pictures taken on it. The trouble is, I didn't know any rich kids like that growing up, and if I had, they certainly wouldn't have invited me to their party.

Karen would have been invited to such a party, but that's not where she got her picture, either.

13

It's always fun when new people show up at the house and admire these photos. They usually make some kind of comment like, "I didn't know you guys grew up together," and they're always surprised to learn that we didn't meet until high school. That's when we laugh and tell them the story.

Though Karen and I went to different schools, we grew up in the same neighborhood in Amarillo, Texas. One day after school I heard a knock on the door and went to answer it. There was a truck and a trailer parked down the street and a couple of guys walking door-to-door with this awesome brown and white Shetland pony in tow. I poked my head out the screen door and one of them said, "Hey, kid, how'd you like to have your picture taken on this horse?"

I thought to myself, *Are you kidding?* I was down the front steps and climbing on board faster than a mouse in a cat store. It never occurred to me that there might be financial ramifications for my parents. I assumed they were just a couple of nice guys with a cool horse. My dad wasn't too happy when the pictures arrived and he got the bill.

That same day, these guys also made their way over to Karen's street, and her parents were thrilled at the opportunity, though they obviously took the time to comb her hair and primp her up a bit before setting her on the saddle. So now we have these two great pictures in our home to confuse visitors.

I love these pictures almost as much as I love telling that story. And not just because of how cute Karen looks in a cowboy hat. I love them because they remind me of a time when life was much simpler and more innocent. As I look at these photos, a flood of memories comes to mind. Memories of my mom and dad and our small house on Lometa Street, right next to Fleetwood Park.

I remember playing ball in the street with my two older brothers, Damien and Lucifer (actually, their names are Randy and Mike). I remember walking to school every day with my friends, then walking home afterward, always taking the longest possible route, looking for mischief along the way. Those days are long gone, but the memories are still fresh in my mind. And they come flooding back each time I walk past these two faded photos.

There's another picture in our home that brings back memories just as fond and even more tender. It's a photo of my granddad, "Papaw." I loved Papaw and spent just about every summer vacation on his farm. He and my grandmother, "Mamaw," would open their home to my brothers and me and then spend all summer just loving on us, feeding us big helpings of bacon, eggs, and biscuits for breakfast, letting us ride on their tractor as they worked the land. Some of my fondest childhood memories were built on Papaw's farm.

But there's another memory tied to Papaw's photo. A traumatic one. Papaw was a chain smoker, and it caught up with him at the age of sixty-three. He died of a massive heart attack, far sooner than he should have died. I was just nineteen at the time and wasn't ready to let him go.

Standing in front of Papaw's casket as they lowered him into the ground was one of the saddest moments of my life. Still to this day the memory haunts me. I wish I'd had more time to spend with him, more days to hang out with him on the farm, to laugh with him as we walked along the road, to learn from him. More moments of sitting next to him at the kitchen table, listening to the stories of his youth. Even now I'd give anything to have one more afternoon with Papaw. I'm convinced that he'll be the first one waiting for me at the Pearly Gates when I pass over, and what a reunion that's going to be.

My Favorite Photo

There's one more photo in our home that makes my heart sing. This one brings back the happiest memories of all. It's our wedding photo. Karen and I are standing side by side, she looking radiant as ever in her beautiful white dress and holding a big bouquet of flowers. And me standing in my black suit with a goofy grin and a head full of stringy blond hair, like a dork who just won the bride lottery.

This photo means more to me than any possession we own. First, because it reminds me of our wedding day, the happiest day of my life. But more importantly, because it symbolizes a time in my life when everything changed for the better. As I look at this photo I'm reminded not only of the day we married, but of the days leading up to it and the moment I nearly lost her.

Just a week before our wedding, Karen broke up with me. I had been living a wild and immoral lifestyle while still trying to convince her that I was a decent person. I'm not sure why she stayed with me, but the closer our wedding day came, the more she knew she couldn't go through with it. My friends were sinful and rowdy, and inside I was just like them. I tried to hide that from Karen, but she saw through the façade.

The day she broke off our wedding was a huge wake-up call to me. I suddenly realized that I was about to lose the only good thing I had going for me—the only friend I had worth keeping. And that realization finally brought me to my knees before God. I repented to God that day and pledged to do whatever it took to stay faithful, if only he would bring Karen back to me. I had prayed to God before, even prayers of repentance, but never with this level of brokenness and shame. It was the moment I finally surrendered myself to his will.

Karen could see my sincerity when I begged her to reconsider. She could tell something in me was different. I didn't deserve her forgiveness, but she forgave me anyway, trusting that I would stay true to my word. She agreed to go through with the wedding, and I did exactly what I told her I would do. I broke off ties with all of my immoral friends and threw myself into the Word, praying daily, pleading with God to make me a better person.

On the day of our wedding I was as frightened as I was excited. I had just lost every friend I had in the world except for Karen and Jesus. I had never before been able to keep a promise—especially a life-changing one—and I honestly didn't know if I could keep this one. But I loved Karen and I loved my Lord, and I was committed to staying faithful to both of them.

It is now over forty years later, and I still have my two best friends—Karen and Jesus. Through all the ups and downs, they've both stayed by my side. God has been with us every step of the way, changing our hearts and making our marriage stronger. It hasn't always been easy—especially the first few years—but I shudder to think where I'd be today without them.

This photo of our wedding day stands as a constant reminder of God's love and faithfulness, even in the midst of my sin and rebellion. It's more than a memory to me; it's my own private stone marker, symbolizing the goodness of God and the journey of faith he continues to lead me through each day.

Stone Markers

That's what photographs are to us. They are tiny bits of remembrance, snapped during a moment of happiness and captured for all time. We display them in an effort to relive the joy, to remember the moment, to somehow reexperience the emotion of the memory.

A mom and daughter are walking along the beach, collecting shells, washing their toes in the tide, laughing and sharing their deepest secrets, bonding spiritually and emotionally. Dad sees the event and scrambles for his camera, aiming it just in time to catch them gazing into each other's eyes, smiling, with the ocean framed in the background. What was intended as a simple snapshot is soon mounted and framed, hung on the wall as a lifelong symbol of love and devotion between a mother and daughter.

A son stands in his cap and gown at a college graduation ceremony, his arm stretched around his father's shoulder. The two pose for a quick picture, and soon the photograph finds its place on the mantel. To most people it is simply another graduation photo. But to the father it is a symbol of profound significance. It reminds him of the years they had together, the many days of mentoring and sacrifice, the times of joy, the moments of frustration, the long nights of prayer on his son's behalf. It is a trophy of triumph and satisfaction. A stone marker of approval, reminding him daily of a daunting task fulfilled.

These small memories have a deep and overwhelming impact on our lives. In many ways they make us who we are. They shape our thoughts and silently guide our lives. They remind us who we are, where we've been, and what we've been through. Moments of pride and joy have a way of burning themselves into the fabric of our hearts, leaving marks of contentment on our spirits. And the more good memories we have, the more likely we are to have a happy and emotionally healthy outlook on life.

The reason such memories affect us so deeply is because you and I are hardwired to remember. It's how God made us. More than that, it's how God *makes* us. How he shapes us. God uses the events and experiences of our lives, not only to draw us to himself, but to push us toward our purpose—toward the people he created us to become.

The images we hang on our walls hang much more prominently on our hearts. And the memories they bring have an eternal impact on our lives.

Photos of Grief

If that's true, then what about the bad memories? What about the moments of pain and disappointment? The times of deep and abiding sadness? The days of trying time and again to succeed, only to end in failure? What about the seasons of sin and rebellion, the times we'd like to forget? What about those memories of abuse or neglect or deep rejection? How do these moments affect our lives?

You and I both know the answer, don't we? Moments of pain can be devastating to the heart and soul. And they can do untold damage to the spirit.

I once heard that it takes ten kind words to undo the pain done by one hurtful and biting comment. I'm not sure who came up with that figure, but I'm convinced it is true. If anything, it's an understatement.

Some good friends of ours are big fans of a program on television called *Intervention*. I've never seen the show, but they've described a number of the episodes to me. The program films real-life interventions, where a group of people confront a friend in an effort to help them overcome a serious problem or dysfunction. Often the person is struggling with an addiction to drugs or alcohol. Sometimes they have a severe eating disorder, like anorexia or bulimia. Other times they are simply unable to process a traumatic event or crisis from their past.

These friends told me about one episode that depicted a girl who refused to swallow. She would chew her food but then spit it out. She had not swallowed in over fourteen years. In order to stay alive, she had taught herself how to inject food directly into her stomach through a tube. The poor girl was dangerously thin and malnourished, and her family was determined to get her help.

Another episode featured a forty-year-old former firefighter named Jeff. He was a decorated hero who had once saved his partner's life. But a traumatic event caused him to start drinking, and soon he lost his job due to several DUIs. His drinking increased, and several times he was rushed to the hospital with severe seizures. His wife and son moved out of the house in frustration, causing him to drink even more. His family finally confronted him on camera in a desperate attempt to get him back on track.

Intervention has been on the air for several years, and each week it chronicles the story of another person suffering through deep pain and addiction. And if you've ever watched the program, you've no doubt noticed an interesting truth. Though the stories are different, there's one common denominator that ties them all together. No matter what addiction these hurting people have, no matter what problem or dysfunction they're struggling with, they can all trace their troubles to a tragic event or circumstance from their past.

Every single story of addiction is somehow rooted in pain. Every dysfunction, no matter how severe, can be traced back to tragedy. Every eating disorder, every case of alcoholism, every emotional disorder they feature has a history of hurt.

I notice that same dynamic in my counseling office. Every person I see with a significant addiction, depression, or other dysfunction—no matter what specific problem they are working through—eventually breaks down in tears as they describe a devastating event or circumstance from their past. I hear stories of abusive fathers, of neglectful mothers, of brutal neighborhood bullies; stories of emotional trauma and heartache, premature deaths, personal rejection, physical and verbal violence, shattered friendships, broken marriages, divorcing parents.

Every person I counsel, without exception, is dealing with some form of deep-seated, unresolved, unprocessed pain from his or her past.

When Pain Lingers

These are not memories we try to hang on to; they are memories that hang on to us. No one displays photographs of grief and misery on their mantel. I've been to a lot of homes, yet I've never once seen a picture of a car accident hanging on a living room wall. I've never seen a devastating diagnosis from the doctor sitting on the shelf, or a pink slip from work framed on an end table. These are events we try to forget, but they remain just the same.

When moments of chaos and confusion come into our lives they have a way of hanging on, of clinging to the core of our consciousness and clawing at the fabric of our emotional health. They take up residence in the darkest corner of our hearts, a place I call the "hurt pocket." And once there, these painful moments set up house, filling the walls with photos of turbulence and turmoil, memories of abuse and neglect and rejection, thoughts of insecurity and self-hate.

The hurt pocket is where unresolved pain goes to hide and gather. And the more space it fills, the more it compromises our mental, emotional, and spiritual health.

It's true that pain is a natural part of life. We all deal with it to varying degrees. People die. Friends leave. Parents make mistakes. Sin brings tragedy into the world on a daily basis, and we're all vulnerable to getting hurt. Much of the grief we experience is manageable. But what about those events that you and I are not equipped to deal with? Those moments of emotional devastation that exceed our ability to cope? The wounding words from someone we love. The father who leaves for no apparent reason. The uncle who suddenly turns into a sexual predator. The accident that leaves us physically or emotionally paralyzed.

These are the moments of pain that begin to collect and build within us, that gather inside the hurt pocket of our souls, leaving our spirits wounded and battered. And the memories they bring have a deep and profound impact on our lives.

Just as the joyous moments we capture on film and hang on the walls of our homes work to lift our spirits, these painful memories work to tear them down. They, too, silently guide our lives, reminding us where we've been and what we've been through. They attach themselves to the fabric of our hearts, leaving marks of insecurity and self-doubt on our spirits. And the more painful memories we have, the harder we have to work to overcome them.

The Healing We Need

There's a phrase that is common in Christian circles. If you've been in the church for any amount of time, you've no doubt heard it. Chances are good you've said it to someone else at one time or another. It's a true phrase that carries lots of wisdom, but also lots of frustration for those who find themselves on the business end of the comment.

It usually comes up in a small group setting where one person finally begins to open up and share some deep-seated feelings of pain or rejection. They'll expose their innermost thoughts to the group, maybe even for the first time, and an awkward silence will follow. Eventually someone will break the silence and say, "Just give your pain to God and he'll bring you comfort."

It's a well-meaning phrase that carries more truth than a mountain of self-help books, but the words can often bring more pain than peace. A person immersed in hurt has no doubt tried to give their pain to God, over and over again, yet still carries it deep inside. To someone who has spent countless nights in prayer, pleading with God to heal their wounded spirit, a comment like this can feel devastating.

If you've found yourself on this page, I'm guessing you understand exactly what I mean. Chances are good you've heard that phrase before, maybe more than a few times. You've been carrying unresolved pain in your heart for longer than you can remember, and you've lost countless hours of sleep praying for relief, yet nothing seems to work.

If I'm right, I encourage you to stay with me as we explore a solution together.

We'll begin by helping to shine a gentle light inside the hurt pocket of your heart, exploring the deep, dark places where pain has gone to hide and fester. We'll expose the pictures of grief and sorrow that hang on the inner walls of your spirit, and perhaps even help you find a name for your pain.

Once there, we'll take a firsthand look at how the enemy works to keep wounds fresh and memories painful. Satan is the father of lies, and he uses grief and misery to keep us in emotional and spiritual bondage. I call Satan the "Hurt Whisperer," because wherever there is pain, you can bet he is there, scheming and plotting, whispering his lies into the core of our hearts and minds. Satan is sly and stealthy, and he relies on his ability to remain under the radar. His voice is not an audible one, but it is always there, always working to tear us down and separate us from God.

Finally, we'll explore some concrete things you and I can do in order to give God complete access to our pain. Only then can he bring the healing we need.

Turns out our friends were right all along. What you and I most need to do is give our pain to God and let him bring comfort. Like most truths of the Christian walk, however, giving our pain to God is a process, not a singular event. And that's a journey best taken together.

―――――――――――――――――― *Takeaway*―――――――――――――――――

- Most of us take photographs to capture those happy and cherished moments in our lives. These photographs remind us who we are, where we've been, and what we've been through.

- Just like the photographs that fill the walls of our homes, the memories that fill our hearts—both pleasant and painful ones—shape our thoughts and silently guide our lives.

- Most of us struggle with unprocessed pain from our past. And these moments of pain begin to collect and gather within the hurt pocket of our spirits. Almost all of us are carrying unresolved pain in our hearts, and the only way to find true healing is to learn how to give our pain to God.

PART 1

The Hurt Pocket

Mental pain is less dramatic than physical pain, but it is more common and also more hard to bear.

—*Dr. R. Havard, in C. S. Lewis,* The Problem of Pain

I am overwhelmed with troubles and my life draws near to death. I am counted among those who go down to the pit; I am like one without strength.

—*Psalm 88:3–4*

—2—

Defining Moments

Most people have not suffered a severe trauma, but everyone has been wounded at some level.

—Edward M. Smith

Whenever I speak on the topic of the hurt pocket, I almost always begin with a simple question. I ask, "How many of you would say you've experienced an event in your life that was emotionally devastating? Something so wounding that it actually altered your personality—maybe even your future?" Without exception, nearly every hand in the room goes up. It never fails, whether I'm speaking to a crowd of five hundred or five thousand.

I then ask a follow-up question: "How many would say this painful issue has been resolved?" This time the response is entirely different. Sometimes a smattering of hands will go up here and there, but the vast majority of those in attendance remain completely silent.

It's a simple exercise and not very scientific, but it serves well to illustrate two important truths.

The first is, *life hurts*. We are all touched by pain and heartache, and often that pain is so devastating, so traumatic, so profoundly wounding that it alters the fabric of our emotional health. In some cases the pain is so unbearable that it redirects the very course of our lives, changing the face of our future.

The second truth is just as sobering: *The pain we experience is seldom resolved.* Few of us are equipped to properly process the hurts we experience, so they remain buried deep within the hurt pocket of our spirits.

To varying degrees, we have all been battered by the storms of humanity. And the wounds we carry affect every area of our lives: our families, our friends, our marriage, our children, our faith, even our relationship with God.

I can look back on my own life and see several traumatic events that wounded me deeply—far deeper than I could have imagined at the time. Most of these events seemed rather insignificant, even commonplace; yet they inflicted emotional and spiritual damage that surfaced in my adult life. These inner wounds affected my life and marriage in a way that I never thought possible. Some of them I still carry.

A Story of Pain

One such wound wasn't so much a specific event as it was a series of hurtful experiences over a period of several years. It began during the summer of my fifth-grade year.

I attended Paramount Terrace Elementary at the time—the same school my brothers had attended before moving on to Crockett Junior High. It was where all my friends went, and I had spent much of the summer dreaming about finally being a sixth-grader. An upperclassman. Everyone knows that sixth-graders rule the roost in grade school.

Then one day, just a few weeks before the end of summer vacation, my parents sat me down and explained that someone in the school district had redrawn the boundary lines, and I was being transferred to Coronado Elementary. I was devastated. I told them I didn't want to go to Coronado, that all my friends were at Paramount Terrace, and that it wasn't fair to make me move just before my sixth-grade year. They tried their best to calm me down, but it didn't help. I was inconsolable.

I started crying and couldn't stop. I ran to my room and bawled well into the evening hours, then cried myself to sleep. I'm sure my parents thought I was just overreacting, but I was truly overcome with grief. I couldn't imagine being yanked away from my friends for no good reason, just because some pinhead on the school board decided to redraw the school map. It seemed completely unfair.

My parents were so distressed by my reaction that they actually went to the school administration building to see if an exception could be made, but it didn't help. They were told the decision had been made and nothing more could be done. Boundaries are boundaries, so I would just have to get over it and plan to attend Coronado.

I don't remember how many nights I cried myself to sleep over the next few weeks, only that I couldn't seem to get past it. The whole thing felt like a monumental act of injustice, and I was determined to fight it.

Then one morning, about a week before school was to start, I came up with a plan. A brilliant plan. One that would fix everything. And suddenly my attitude completely changed. I went to breakfast with a smile on my face and a skip in my step. My mom and dad immediately noticed the difference. "You certainly look happy this morning," my mother said to me. I just smiled and went about my day. I knew exactly what needed to be done.

The first day of school finally came, and I woke up bright and early. I put on my favorite shirt and jeans, got my school supplies together, then cheerfully sat at the breakfast table. "You know, you're really taking this well," my mother said. "I'm proud of you."

"I am taking it well," I told her.

After breakfast I gathered my things, kissed her good-bye, and headed down the sidewalk. Only instead of turning the corner toward Coronado I walked straight toward Paramount Terrace, where I belonged. I thought to myself, *With all those kids running around, they'll never even notice me. I'll just go to school with my friends, like I always have. Once I'm there they'll have to keep me. That's their job!* It was a brilliant plan—and so simple. I wondered why I hadn't thought of it sooner.

I got to school and found a seat in the sixth-grade classroom, right next to a handful of my friends. "Hey, Evans, I thought they moved you to Coronado," one friend said when he saw me.

"Nope," I told him. "I go to school here." I was sure I was home free. All I had to do was keep a low profile for a few days and everything would work out fine.

It only took a few minutes into the first period for the teacher to notice me. I saw her walking toward the back of the room, right where I was sitting, so I quickly took out a piece of paper and started writing. *If she thinks I'm studying, maybe she'll move on to the next kid,* I thought. But it didn't work.

"Hello, Jimmy. How are you?" she asked.

"I'm fine. Thank you for asking." I tried my best to sound inconspicuous.

"Jimmy, I'm afraid I don't have you on the roll for my class."

"Well, I'm here," I told her. I figured all she had to do was go back to her seat and pencil my name on her sheet and everything would be fixed. But she didn't budge.

"I think you might need to go down to the office and get permission to be in my class. Why don't you do that?"

I knew this wasn't good. I slowly gathered my things together and made the long walk toward the principal's office. I was still convinced I could pull this off. The secretary's name was Mrs. Mullins, and she had always liked me. *Mrs. Mullins will let me stay*, I thought. *She's a nice lady. Surely she won't send me away.*

I walked up to her desk, and with all the confidence I could muster said, "Mrs. Mullins, my teacher doesn't have me in her records and she needs me to get some information from you so I can go back and be in her class." Then I gave her my handsomest smile.

She looked through some paperwork, then back at me. "Aren't you supposed to be going to Coronado this year, Jimmy?"

"No ma'am," I said. "I go to school here."

Again she glanced down at her papers. "Well, Mr. Thorn will be here in a few minutes. Why don't you take a seat and wait for him?"

This wasn't going as I had expected. Now I had to speak to the principal, and I was scared to death of Mr. Thorn. I took a seat and waited, hoping maybe he wouldn't show. But within a few minutes he came through the door, giving me a quick double take as he walked by. Mrs. Mullins met him at the door and whispered something into his ear, then the two of them slipped into his office and closed the door. This was getting worse by the minute.

After a short while the two emerged. The second I saw Mr. Thorn's face I knew my plan had failed. I'll never forget the look of compassion in his eyes as he asked me to step into his office.

"Jimmy," he said, leaning across his desk with his hands folded, "I'm so sorry, but we're going to have to send you to Coronado. I know you don't want to go there, but there's nothing I can do."

I cried and pleaded with him to let me stay, but to no avail. I honestly wondered if Mr. Thorn didn't feel worse about the whole thing than I did. I had no idea school principals could be so sympathetic. He handed me a tissue, then the two of us headed toward the parking lot so he could drive me to Coronado.

A Year of Persecution

My sixth-grade year at Coronado Elementary was the worst year of my life. I hated literally every minute of it, and I was determined to let everyone know how miserable I had become. I found myself looking for ways to act out, and I didn't even care when they punished me.

Quite honestly, I had no reason to feel this way. The teachers were much nicer than I had expected, and I made friends easily enough. But I couldn't get past the unfairness of the whole ordeal. All my old friends were at Paramount Terrace, and that's where I should have been. I would go home after school and see my friends from the neighborhood walking home from Paramount Terrace, laughing and joking with each other, and it killed me to think that I had been left out of all the fun. Why was I the only one being picked on? What did I do wrong? I was the most persecuted sixth-grader on the planet, and I made sure everyone knew about it—especially my parents.

At the end of the year, I assumed I would be forced to attend Stephen F. Austin Junior High, since that's where the Coronado students were expected to go. I wasn't happy about that, either. But during the summer months my parents got the news that I would be allowed to attend Crockett Junior High. Someone had discovered a loophole in the zoning rules, and since my brothers were already attending Crockett, I would be allowed to cross the boundary lines if I wanted. It was the best news I could imagine. Crockett was where all my old friends would be going, and I could finally be reunited with them. To a victimized thirteen-year-old, this was the equivalent of winning the state lottery. I was beside myself and couldn't wait for school to begin.

For the next two years I went to Crockett, and they were some of the happiest years of my life. I started getting better grades, simply because my attitude had changed so drastically. I also developed a love for sports. I went out for the football team and did really well. All my friends were on the team, and we spent every afternoon hanging out together after practice, talking football and girls and all the other things that "cool school jocks" talk about.

In time I had all but forgotten those horrible months of mistreatment I suffered at the hands of the school board during my sixth-grade year. Life was back on track.

More Injustice

Then one day, just a few weeks before I was to start ninth grade, my parents once again came to me with grim news. My dad was carrying a note from the school administrator. They explained to me that the school board had voted again to redraw the boundaries, and this time they did away with any exemptions. My loophole had been closed, and I was being transferred to Stephen F. Austin for my ninth-grade year.

At that moment, all my feelings of anger and frustration came flooding back, this time with an even greater sense of resentment. *They can't do this to me!* I thought. *Not again!*

I could feel the rage building in my spirit. I said to my parents, "You can't let them do this to me! You know this isn't fair! Can't you do something about it? Please don't let them do this to me again!"

I've always known that if you really want to get a rise out of parents, all you have to do is mistreat one of their kids. Even a mountain lion knows better than to come between a mama bear and her cubs. I was surprised at my parents' response. They seemed more incensed than I was.

The next day my dad went down to the school board and had a talk with the people in charge. I'm not sure what he said or who he talked to, but he let them know he wasn't very happy. Eventually they came to a compromise. I would be allowed to attend Crockett, but technically I would still be seen as a student of Stephen F. Austin. That meant I could go to classes at Crockett, but I couldn't play sports. My dad wasn't happy with the arrangement, but it was the best he could do.

I was thrilled when my dad told me the news, but still a bit confused. I couldn't understand why I wouldn't be allowed to play football. I was a good player and a valuable part of the team. It felt more like a punishment than a compromise—like some random rule a school administrator came up with in order to get back at me for fighting the system. The proposal never did feel fair to me, but at least I could finish school with my friends.

At the time, I didn't realize how hard it would be to sit on the sidelines while my friends were allowed to play. Every time someone would ask me why I wasn't on the field I had to explain the whole thing to them, and with each new telling, the rule seemed even more unreasonable. I always put on a good face and tried to make the best of it, but inside I was angrier than ever. *Who are they to tell me I can't play football? What gives them the right to try to control my life?*

Day by day the resentment in my spirit grew deeper. And that resentment was aimed at every person in the school system, from my teachers to the school principal, even the guys who mowed the lawn and kept the building clean. Anyone who seemed to be in a position of authority began to feel like an enemy. I honestly didn't want to have a bad year; I just couldn't seem to get past the unfairness of sitting on the sidelines week after week. Especially since no one had ever given me a good reason for this seemingly random rule.

The Final Straw

Junior high football games were held on Thursday afternoons, and I always looked forward to the days we played Fannin Junior High, one of the neighboring schools in our district. I had lots of friends at Fannin, which always made the rivalry more fun—especially when we won.

During one such game against Fannin, I was rooting hard for our team, losing my voice from screaming, and I decided to make a quick trip to the vending truck for a Coke. On the way, I happened to pass by a few of the Fannin cheerleaders. Actually, I had to go a little out of the way in order to "happen" by them, but it was worth the trip because they saw me and called me over to say hi. A couple of them were friends of mine from grade school, though I don't remember them being quite as cute in the second grade. I sauntered over to where they were standing and spent a few minutes flirting with them.

Eventually they had to get back to cheering, so I bought my snacks from the vending truck, then made my way back to my seat to finish watching the game.

During first period the next morning, my teacher handed me a note saying that the principal wanted to see me. This was never a good sign, and all the way to his office my mind raced, wondering what I had done wrong. Or at least, what he had found out about.

I was stunned to see the principal standing in front of his desk holding a paddle when I walked in. "Jimmy, come in and bend over," he said. "Time to get your licks."

My jaw dropped to the floor. "Why? What did I do?"

"You know what you did," he answered.

"No, I don't." In most cases I would have known exactly what I was in trouble for, but this time I honestly had no clue. And I certainly wasn't about to confess to something before finding out what he knew.

"Yesterday at the game," he said. "I saw you talking to the Fannin cheerleaders. You know it's against the rules to fraternize with the other team. Now bend over and take your punishment."

I didn't know what "fraternize" meant; I just knew I wasn't guilty of it. All I did was visit with a few friends during the game. How could that have gotten me into trouble?

The more I protested the angrier he got, so I bent over the desk and took my licks. Four times he swatted me on the bottom, each one a little harder than the last. I was sure he enjoyed every second of it.

I left his office that day without saying a word. My jaw clenched tight with anger, and my shoulders stiffened. It's a good thing I bit my tongue, because there's no telling what I might have said. I can't remember the last time I felt so enraged. So filled with bitterness and anger.

Something deep in my spirit completely shut down that day. I was devastated. I don't even remember walking back to class, only that I vowed in my heart to get even. They were going to pay for all the things they had done to me. All the years of injustice, of yanking me around for no reason, all the random rules they made me obey, all the idiotic boundary lines, all the weeks of forcing me to sit on the sidelines for no good reason. Someone was going to pay.

Defining Moments

We can all look back over our past and pinpoint a handful of life-defining moments—those specific events or circumstances that somehow rattle us to the core of our being, knocking us off-center. They are moments that seem to come out of nowhere, that catch us off-guard, and once played out they leave a wake of confusion and doubt.

For me, this simple event became one of those moments. It certainly wasn't the first—or last—time I had gotten licks from the principal, but something about this particular incident seemed so profoundly unreasonable that it shook me to the very foundation. If it had been just this one act of injustice I probably would have laughed it off and gone on my way. But after so many years of feeling mistreated, so many moments of anger and resentment toward those in authority, something within me finally snapped.

I went back to the classroom that day, gathered my rowdy friends in a small circle, and said, "I'm going to challenge you guys to a contest. Starting right now, let's see who can get into the most trouble before the end of the year. I'll bet I can get more licks than any one of you."

Of course, they were all for it. "Let's do it," they said. "Let's see who can cause the most trouble!"

That's what they said, but then fifteen-year-old boys say a lot when they're bragging to their friends. I'm not sure any of them realized just how serious I was.

Takeaway

- Almost every one of us has suffered wounds in life that are emotionally devastating—events so tragic that they affect our emotional health and often redirect the course of our future.

- There are two truths about life that I believe are universal: (1) We have all been touched by pain and heartache. (2) The painful experiences we suffer are seldom resolved.

- At a very young age, I experienced a series of painful events that had a marked impact on my heart and personality. Almost all of us have painful experiences that stay with us well into our adult years.

—3—

Inner Vows

The events of childhood do not pass, but repeat themselves like seasons of the year.

—Eleanor Parjeon

Typically, we hurt others most deeply in the areas of our deepest wounding.

—Sandra D. Wilson

When pain comes into our lives, it leaves us with many options. But one thing it never leaves us is unscathed. Pain has to be dealt with. You can't just walk through it and come out the other side unaffected.

When you get a cut on your leg, you have a visible, open wound that needs tending, otherwise it might get infected. So we immediately tend to the wound. We douse it in alcohol, salve it with antibiotic, and then cover it with a bandage in order to help it heal.

The problem with inner pain is that you can't see it. The cut is just as deep and destructive, but you don't always know it's there. So you pretend it doesn't exist, or at least push it back into the deep recesses. You try to live as if nothing happened. But the pain is very real and can easily lead to bitterness and resentment. It begins to seethe and fester, seeping into the heart and spirit. The infection spreads because the wound hasn't been dealt with properly.

Inner pain is far more dangerous and toxic than any outer wound we can suffer. Inner pain leaves us emotionally scarred and damaged, causing us to act out in ways we would otherwise never consider.

That day so many years ago, as I was making the long walk from the principal's office back to my classroom, after getting licks I didn't deserve from a man who seemed to enjoy making my life miserable, I could feel the welts from his switch stinging my bottom side. But that pain would soon go away. The most devastating wound was festering deep inside my spirit, hidden from sight. The unfairness of it all was more than I could emotionally process.

And the pain had to be dealt with. So I dealt with it the only way my damaged heart could manage. I began to rebel.

Birth of a Rebel

Standing in the classroom that day surrounded by my band of misfit friends, my teeth still clenched in anger and my jaw set squarely on revenge, I'm not sure anyone understood the depth of my rage as I challenged them to that twisted contest. But I had never been more serious. I was intent on making life miserable for every person in the school who ever did me wrong.

For the rest of that year I was a living terror. I acted out at every possible opportunity. I began smoking and drinking and cursing. I lost interest in school and sports, and instead spent my time looking for ways to get into trouble. Every teacher in the school knew me by name and watched my every move. Some days I spent more time in the principal's office than I did in the classroom, and I didn't even care. I got more licks than any kid in the school, hands down, and with each swat my anger and resolve grew even deeper.

The last week of school, I remember standing in front of the principal's desk, my backside still stinging from another round of licks, and just as I turned to head back to my classroom the principal looked me in the eye and said, "Evans, if you see my face one more time before school is out I will expel you and see that you never get to go to high school! Do you understand me?"

His face was red with anger, and his finger shook as he pointed it right at my face. I had never seen him this angry.

But I was determined not to flinch. I stared back at him with all the wrath and intimidation I could muster. It was my Dirty Harry moment.

"Do you understand me, young man?" he said again. "Do not test me on this! I promise you will never see high school if I see you in here one more time!"

Still today I'm surprised that I didn't talk back. But I could see in his eyes that I had pushed him one rung too far, so I bit my tongue and decided to lay low the next few days.

Needless to say, I won the contest with my friends. I may have been the most unruly, disruptive ninth-grade kid Amarillo had ever seen.

I'm not proud of it today, but I certainly was at the time. I had done exactly what I set out to do. And I couldn't wait to continue my successful run in high school.

High School

Several months later, when the summer break was over, I showed up for my first day at Tascosa High School with a scowl on my face, a chip on my shoulder, and a pack of Marlboro cigarettes in my pocket. I was a big kid—actually a huge kid for my age—so I looked more like a senior than an incoming freshman. And I was intent on maintaining my reputation as a troublemaker.

Since I was such a large kid and a good athlete, the football coach called me at home and asked if I was planning to try out for the team. "We could really use you," he told me.

But I had no interest in being helpful, especially to teachers. So I told him no. It was a foolish act of pride that I regretted for the next three years, but I was too stubborn to change my mind.

My grades reflected my apathy. I don't remember once taking a book home to study. I knew I needed to pass in order to get through high school, so when tests came around I'd crack open a book in study hall and read just enough to get by, but that was all the effort I was willing to give. There were 770 kids in our graduating class, and I placed somewhere around 550. I graduated in the bottom 30 percent of the class, and was honestly surprised I did that well. I'm not sure how the bottom two hundred kids made it through, because my grades were so low I almost didn't get to graduate.

I got into more trouble during those three years than I thought humanly possible. It seems that every week I was discovering bigger and better ways to make life miserable for everyone around me, especially the teachers. I got so many licks in high school that I wondered why the principal didn't just pencil me into his daily calendar. My backside had more callouses than a rancher's hands. I was a walking, breathing ball of terror, and teachers lived in fear of having me assigned to their classrooms.

In fact, one teacher was so traumatized by my behavior that she quit teaching school altogether. I didn't know that until years later, while I was serving as senior pastor of Trinity Fellowship in Amarillo. One day after church a member and her husband came up to meet me, and after exchanging a few pleasantries, she said, "Did you know my mother was one of your teachers in high school?"

I instantly broke out in a cold sweat. "No, I didn't know that," I said.

She told me her name, and I immediately remembered. Then she said, "Mom told us that you were such an unbearable student that she actually quit teaching the year you graduated. She said she couldn't take it anymore."

All I could do was feign a smile and apologize. We had a good laugh, but I couldn't have been more embarrassed.

My Greatest Regret

As I look back on those years, I'm stunned that I allowed my anger to grow so intense. I may have acted tough, but deep inside I was miserable. And the more I acted out, the more depressed and angry I became. I'm certain I was one of the unhappiest kids in school, but I never let it show. I simply gritted my teeth and looked for more ways to feed my inner rage.

Today I'm ashamed of the way I allowed myself to act. High school is supposed to be a time of making new friends and enjoying your youth. A time of developing fond memories and preparing for the future. But my high school memories are nothing like that. All I remember are thoughts of bitterness, resentment, and rebellion.

One of my greatest regrets in life is wasting my high school years on anger and rebellion. My goal was to get back at those I thought had wronged me, but all I succeeded in doing was losing out on what should have been some of the happiest years of my life.

Whenever I see a young high school kid showing obvious signs of rebellion, it's all I can do to keep from grabbing them by the shirt collar and saying to them, "Listen, don't do this to yourself! Don't throw away the best years of your life on resentment and anger. Don't give others that much power over your life. You will never have another opportunity to be this young and vibrant and carefree. I promise, when you are my age, you will regret every moment you've spent in anger and rebellion. You will regret every night you spent sitting at home sulking and scheming instead of making good friends and having fun!"

Today I can look back and see that no one was ever out to get me. As much as I enjoyed playing the role of martyr, no one intentionally set out to make my life miserable. Schools have rules for a reason, and sometimes school boundaries need to be redrawn. I'm sure that my name never once came up when those things were being discussed.

Every time I got licks, I deserved them. The teachers and principals were great people who were simply doing their jobs. In every case, I was the one at fault. But at the time none of that ever crossed my mind. All I could think about was getting even for the injustice I had suffered at the hands of school officials. And because of that, I became a miserable person.

The Problem with Inner Vows

That's how pain works. When we are wounded by those around us, even if those wounds are unintentional, the pain settles into our spirits.

It seethes deep inside, and like a cancerous tumor it begins to slowly spread and reproduce. Before we know it, the infection is affecting every other area of our lives.

And these wounds inevitably set up shop in the hurt pocket. They go there to find refuge and consolation, but all they find is more pain and misery.

Wounds that are tucked away lead to inner thoughts that are corrosive. Sometimes these thoughts turn to vows. Inner vows are more common than many of us might believe. We've all made them at one time or another.

"No one will ever treat me like that again."

"I'll never let myself be poor."

"I'll never force my children to go to church."

"I'll never let anyone break my heart like that again."

Inner vows are damaging promises we make in order to comfort ourselves in times of pain, frustration, or difficulty. And they are never healthy.

The damaging inner vows I made as a young man were deeply misguided and irrational, and based more on perception than reality, but that didn't occur to me at the time. I was simply dealing with the pain the only way I knew how. I began acting out in rebellion and disobedience. And I began looking for ways to get into trouble, because trouble was my way of coping with the pain.

Inner vows do far more than simply undermine our emotional stability. They also do untold damage to our relationships, including our relationship with God. They cause us to act out in ways that are not only unhealthy, but counter to God's Word.

There are three major problems with inner vows:

They Are Sinful

Jesus tells us, "Do not swear an oath. . . . All you need to say is simply 'Yes' or 'No'; anything beyond this comes from the evil one"

(Matt. 5:34, 37). As God's children, we have surrendered our rights of self-determination. We are called to be subject to God in every area of our lives. And any area that is operating under an inner vow is not submitted to God. That's why inner vows cause so many problems. Because Jesus is not Lord of those areas—we are. And wherever Jesus is not Lord, Satan is in control. Inner vows don't just cause us to sin; they are inherently sinful, in and of themselves.

They Cause Us to Overreact

Often inner vows cause us to act out in ways that are irrational and absurd—even "crazy." Inner vows can make people do things that are completely out of character for them. A man who says to himself, "I'll never be poor again" will often do everything in his power to keep that inner vow. He will go to foolish extremes in the area of money. He may begin hoarding cash in a secret account, or storing gold and silver coins in a safe that only he knows about. And he may do so even at the expense of his family's basic needs.

They Become the Guiding Force of Our Lives

Because inner vows are rooted in such deep pain and turmoil, they can easily become the most powerful and guiding force of our lives. Like a runaway train on a broken track, they set us on a course toward almost certain disaster. And few of us are equipped with the emotional skills to stop it.

Inner vows have a way of taking over our better judgment, causing us to act out in ways that are not only damaging but highly absurd and entirely unreasonable. We begin to do things that no sane person would do.

A Guiding Force

As a child, I had very few clothes to wear. For many years I had only two shirts and one pair of jeans, and I remember being deeply embarrassed about it. Most of my friends had closets full of clothes, yet I wore pretty much the same thing to school every day. I have a vivid memory of standing in front of my closet one day as a child and saying to myself, "When I grow up and have money of my own, I'm going to have nice clothes!"

I had no idea at the time how much this simple, seemingly harmless inner vow would affect my future. But thirty years later, during an argument with Karen, she said to me, "Jimmy, why are you such a clothes horse? You have way too many clothes, but you keep buying more!"

Her comment surprised me, but as I stood looking in my closet I realized that she was right. I had more clothes than I could possibly need, and I had no idea why. And I couldn't deny how strange it was that I would spend so much of our money on clothes when I wasn't really into fashion. I had clothes in my closet that still had the tags on, shirts I hadn't even worn, yet I was still buying new clothes.

Suddenly I remembered that inner vow I had made to myself as a child, and I realized what a guiding force it had been in my life for so many years. It was an inner vow that needed to be broken, so I committed that day to breaking it.

That's how inner vows work. They guide us in ways that are completely irrational and unhealthy. And they control us in ways that only God should be allowed to do.

Damaged Relationships

A man who grows up wounded by a critical and controlling mother may promise to never again allow himself to be dominated by a woman. So he learns to hide his feelings from others. When he marries, he becomes closed off and distant from his wife. He guards his heart and refuses to talk about things that bother him. As a result, their marriage becomes cold and meaningless.

A young girl who grows up in an emotionally abusive family may make an inner vow to never again let herself be hurt by another person. She promises herself that she will never allow anyone to yell at her or put her down. And in order to fulfill her vow, she herself becomes the abuser. She starts lashing out at the first sign of trouble, taking control of every situation in order to maintain the upper hand. Soon she becomes the very person she vowed to steer clear of.

Unhealthy inner vows are not only a powerful force in life, but they can easily become a crippling obsession. They can guide us in ways that make it nearly impossible to develop and maintain a truly healthy relationship.

When you see a bully picking on smaller kids on the playground, often what you're witnessing is a child who has been deeply wounded by others—perhaps an angry father or mother or older sibling. So they act out their rage by picking on those who are smaller. They learn to control their world through brute force and intimidation. And this need to dominate carries over into every relationship they have, including their future marriage.

Inner vows can also do untold damage to our relationship with God.

I know one family with three children who suffered through an enormous amount of pain a few years back. All families struggle with some degree of hardship, but this particular family had far more than their share. And the parents were completely unequipped to help their children process the struggles they were experiencing. Because of it, all three children were left to deal with the pain on their own.

The oldest child acted out in rebellion. He began revolting against authority, getting into trouble at every opportunity. Like me, he processed his pain by trying to get even with those who had hurt him. Today, at the age of forty, he is still rebelling, still acting out in anger and hostility. And his family has suffered even greater turmoil because of it.

The second child began acting out in hate. He hated everyone he came into contact with and simply withdrew into his own world of bitterness and isolation. Hatred is a habit that's hard to break. Still today he keeps to himself and has little to do with the rest of the family. He despises the world for what it did to him and his family, and as a result he lives a miserable existence.

The third child, who was the only daughter, turned her anger inward and became filled with self-hatred and insecurity. She became one of the most shy and introverted people I'd ever met. She could hardly speak in the presence of others and struggled much of her life with deep-seated feelings of anxiety and self-doubt. Thankfully she eventually turned to God and is now working through her insecurities. But because of her past, she still has a lot of pain and bitterness to work through in order to find healing.

All three children dealt with their pain by making unhealthy inner vows. They made internal promises that were designed to keep them from getting hurt in the future. But all it did was make things worse.

Healing for a Heart of Stone

At its core, an inner vow is nothing more than an emotional and spiritual breach of trust. It is you and me saying to God, "I don't think you're big enough to protect me. I don't think you're loving enough to heal my pain. I don't think you're good enough to get me through this."

We don't trust God to be there when we need him most, so we decide to take control of our own destiny. Instead of trusting God with our hurts, we look for strength from within. We take matters into our own hands because we've somehow convinced ourselves that God doesn't care enough to help.

The hurt pocket begins as a place to hide our pain from others. But it quickly becomes our way of attempting to conceal our pain from God.

As a wounded teenager, I became an expert at hiding my pain. On the outside I appeared as tough as nails and as strong as an ox. Most of my friends would have told you that I was a confident and self-assured kid who never let anything bother me. I came across as a happy and assertive young man with a healthy self-esteem. But that was just a ruse. On the inside I was deeply insecure and vulnerable. My heart was scarred and weak and writhing in pain. I was severely wounded, and I made it my full-time job to keep that fact hidden from others.

Even as a young married man I carried that pain with me. And it very nearly destroyed our marriage. Karen is a patient and kind woman, and she tried her best to help me open up, but I couldn't do it. I would shut down at the first sign of trouble. I became an emotional bully as a way of hiding my pain even further.

It was only when I decided to give my pain to God once and for all that I was able to begin the long road of emotional and spiritual healing. I finally raised the white flag of surrender and allowed God access into the deepest, darkest, most hidden corners of my spirit. And only then was God able to begin healing the inner wounds that had brought so much pain and chaos into my life and marriage.

God tells us through the prophet Ezekiel, "I will give you a new heart and put a new spirit in you; I will remove from you your heart of stone and give you a heart of flesh" (Ezek. 36:26).

Inner vows create in us a *heart of stone*, and God is able to remove the hardness from our hearts if we allow him. God promises a new heart and a new spirit. He replaces a heart of stone with a *heart of flesh*.

To those who are struggling with damaging inner vows, know that there is life after pain. That's the message of God's transforming Spirit.

To anyone struggling with internal turmoil, to anyone who has been deeply wounded by those around them, to any woman who has been the victim of emotional or physical abuse, to any man who struggles with thoughts of rage and rebellion, to any person who fights daily to break free from the damaging and unhealthy inner vows that have held them hostage, know that you can find freedom from the pain.

Take it from someone who knows firsthand, someone who understands inner turmoil intimately. Inner vows can destroy you from the inside out. They will compromise every relationship you try to maintain, extinguish the happiness you try to find, crush the dreams you have for your life, and make it almost impossible for you to develop a deep trust in God.

And the only way to freedom is to surrender your inner vows to God. To give him complete and total access to those painful parts of yourself and let him do a miracle in your heart and spirit.

Let God take away your heart of stone and replace it with a heart of flesh. Trust God with the pain of your past that has turned to anger and resentment. Let him give you a new heart and a new spirit.

He's waiting for you to take the first step toward freedom.

Takeaway

- The problem with inner pain is that we don't always know it is there, and so the wounds go untended. Instead of dealing with these wounds, we stuff them into the hurt pocket of our spirits, where they grow and fester.

- Unprocessed pain often causes us to make damaging inner vows. These vows are intended to protect us from future pain, but all they do is cause even greater pain and heartache.

- At its core, an inner vow is an emotional and spiritual breach of trust. It is our attempt to maintain control over our lives when we instead should be surrendering every area of our lives to God.

—4—

When Hurt Hides

Pain insists upon being attended to.

—*C. S. Lewis*

Most of us have a picture in our mind's eye of how life is supposed to work. A baby is born into a wonderful Christian family, with a loving, doting mother and a caring father. He comes into the world smiling and laughing, with no emotional or spiritual baggage. And his parents are completely equipped to shepherd him through life.

One day the child gets his first emotional bruise, and his parents immediately tend to his wounded heart. They hug and comfort him until he feels better.

As the boy grows, the emotional attacks to his heart and spirit become even more brutal and severe, but each time his parents are there to help him through. They always know exactly what to say to help him cope and heal.

The boy eventually grows up and has children of his own, and because of his parents' loving care and guidance, he is completely equipped to raise emotionally healthy children. He guides his children through life the same way his parents guided him. Every issue is resolved before it ever has the chance to do irreparable harm.

That's the way life is supposed to work—at least in a perfect world. But for most of us, that's not the reality we've experienced—not even close.

For most of us, life has dealt some devastating blows. We've suffered some overwhelming attacks to our sense of self and emotional abuse that were far more than our parents were capable of shepherding us through.

Most of us have internal wounds that have never been properly dealt with or processed. Some of those wounds are just painful memories, while others may have left us emotionally and spiritually crippled in certain areas of our lives.

Does Time Heal?

There is a famous saying that we've all heard: "Time heals all wounds."

I'm not sure where that phrase came from, but I've known it since I was a child. You probably have too. But is it true that all wounds—both internal and external—heal with the passing of time?

The ancient Greeks had a word they used when confronted with this type of question. The word is *anoisia*. Loosely translated, it means, "Baloney!"

The reality is, when it comes to emotional and spiritual wounds, time heals nothing. In fact, in many cases time only increases the pain.

I once had emotional wounds that were thirty years old, and they felt just as fresh and painful as the day I suffered them. And you have likely experienced the same thing. Any wound that is unresolved and unprocessed remains deep in our hearts and spirits.

Time may blunt the pain or distance us from the memory, but it doesn't heal the wound. The cut is just as open and vulnerable and exposed as it was the day we were hurt. The wound remains in the hurt pocket of our spirits, right where it was the day we stuffed it there.

And the more unprocessed wounds we suffer over the course of time, the more they grow and accumulate within us. By the time many of us reach adulthood, our hurt pockets are filled to the brim with untreated, unresolved emotional pain and baggage. In many ways we are all just walking wounded soldiers, doing the best we can to stay in the battle.

How We Deal with Pain

One thing I've learned in my years as a pastor is that you can't always judge a person's heart by their actions. More often than not, our actions reflect the depth of our pain more than the status of our hearts.

When I see a young wife in my office in tears because she can't seem to open up sexually to her new husband, I never assume it's because she somehow doesn't love him. Her heart wants desperately to let go and enjoy God's gift to them as a couple. It's her pain that's causing her to hold back. Something in her past is refusing to let go, and it causes her to recoil at the first sign of intimacy. Maybe she was sexually or physically abused as a child, or somehow given the message that sex is dirty and wrong. Whatever the cause, she struggles to let go because her pain is holding her heart hostage.

When I see a man struggling with alcoholism, I never assume it's because he has a wicked heart. The bottle is simply his way of salving a deep-seated pain in his spirit. Somewhere along the way his emotional wounds became more than he could bear, so he started drowning his sorrows in alcohol. And he just kept drowning them, until eventually the addiction overtook him. He doesn't drink because he's evil; he drinks because he hurts.

Pain has to be dealt with, one way or another. And left to our own devices, we will almost always deal with it in the wrong way.

In my years as a counselor and pastor, I've identified three primary ways that most of us deal with pain. These are not healthy methods of dealing with pain, but they are common. I've seen the pattern over and over again, both in my own life and in the lives of others. I've also seen these methods through stories and characters in the Bible.

The First Method: *We Medicate*

Perhaps the most common way most of us deal with inner pain is through unhealthy medication. We medicate ourselves with food, drugs, alcohol, sex, or some other type of pleasure that we can pour over the pain to make it feel better. We look for ways to distract ourselves from the hurt we feel so that we don't have to deal with the root cause of our pain.

I recently did an in-depth study of the life of King David, and I'm convinced that this is how he dealt with the pain of his early years.

We all know that David had sexual problems, but I believe he likely had a full-fledged addiction to sex. So intense was his desire for Bathsheba that he actually had her husband killed over the relationship (see 2 Sam. 11).

As king of Israel, he had at least eight wives and ten concubines, maybe more. If that isn't a sign of sexual addiction, I'm not sure what is.

So what caused David's deep need for sexual conquest?

As a young boy, David's family was something of a case study in dysfunction. He was the youngest of eight boys and spent most of his early years in the fields, tending his father's sheep. It was a lonesome job usually reserved for the lowliest child or servant.

When Samuel came to Jesse's house to anoint the new king of Israel, he asked to see all of Jesse's sons, yet Jesse didn't even bother to call David in from the field. One by one he introduced Samuel to his other seven sons, assuming that one of them would be worthy of God's anointing.

After praying over each of the seven boys, Samuel said to Jesse, "The Lord has not chosen these. . . . Are these all the sons you have?"

Jesse answered, "There is still the youngest. He is tending sheep" (see 1 Sam. 16:1–13).

Jesse didn't even refer to David by name. He simply couldn't imagine that his youngest son would be worthy of Samuel's time.

Even after Samuel anointed David, David's brothers continued to reject him. When his three older brothers went to war with Saul's army, they were quickly stopped in their tracks by a giant Philistine named Goliath. So Jesse sent David to bring them food on the front lines of battle. When David's oldest brother, Eliab, saw him, Scripture tells us he "burned with anger" and said to him, "Why have you come down here? And with whom did you leave those few sheep in the wilderness?" (1 Sam. 17:28).

David was continually overlooked and discounted by his family. He was put down and rejected by his father and his brothers. And even Saul, who had always loved and accepted David as his favorite servant, quickly turned on him after he killed Goliath. When he heard the people praising David for his bravery, King Saul became jealous and set out to kill him.

As we see David's early life unfold in the pages of Scripture, we see a picture of deep pain and rejection. He was criticized and undermined by the people he loved the most. The emotional scars he suffered had to be devastating to his self-image. And I believe that because of his wounds, David began to medicate his pain through sexual conquest.

David ultimately turned to God for healing. As we read the Psalms, we see a portrait of a man who loved God with his whole heart, soul, and mind. David obviously learned to give his pain to God, but that wasn't always the case. As a young king, David was deeply wounded, and he tried to heal his pain through unhealthy medication.

How many times have you and I tried to do the same thing?

When it comes to addiction, the way we medicate is never the issue. When a person is addicted to drugs, drugs are never the real problem. The problem is how he or she tries to deal with pain. When we overeat, food is never the heart of the issue. Food is just our way of salving and deflecting the pain in our spirits.

We medicate as a way of redirecting our attention from the true cause of our misery.

The Second Method: *We Motivate*

The second unhealthy way we deal with pain is through motivation. We turn to busyness and driving ambition in order to salve the wounds in our hearts.

Motivation can be positive, but when it is driven by pain and woundedness it can lead to damaging and dysfunctional behavior. Often when you see an overachiever, you are witnessing an attempt to salve a painful heart through success and unhealthy ambition.

This is how I found myself dealing with pain during the early years of our marriage. People who knew me thought I was simply determined to provide well for my family. Intent on making something of myself, I loved the sense of success and accomplishment. But my motive was far from healthy. Inside I was deeply insecure and wounded, and my ambition was simply my way of masking the pain. The more I achieved, the emptier it all felt.

King Solomon was also an unhealthy motivator. During his reign as king of Israel, he accomplished more than either his father, David, or King Saul before him. Solomon was the ultimate overachiever. He set out to make Israel the richest and greatest nation the earth had ever known, and he accomplished that goal.

Listen to how Solomon describes his accomplishments:

> I undertook great projects: I built houses for myself and planted vineyards. I made gardens and parks and planted all kinds of fruit trees in them. I made reservoirs to water groves of flourishing trees. I bought male and female slaves and had other slaves who were born in my house. I also owned more herds and flocks than anyone in Jerusalem before me. I amassed silver and gold for myself, and the treasure of kings and provinces. I acquired male and female singers, and a harem as well—the delights of a man's heart. I became greater by far than anyone in Jerusalem before me. In all this my wisdom stayed with me.
>
> I denied myself nothing my eyes desired;
>   I refused my heart no pleasure.
> My heart took delight in all my labor,
>   and this was the reward for all my toil. (Eccles. 2:4–10)

Solomon became the poster child for success and achievement. He accomplished every goal he set for himself, probably several times over. Yet at the end of his life, as he looked back and saw all that he had done, it left him empty and unfulfilled.

> Yet when I surveyed all that my hands had done
>   and what I had toiled to achieve,
> everything was meaningless, a chasing after the wind;
>   nothing was gained under the sun. (2:11)

So what drove Solomon to such runaway ambition? What caused him to become such a world-class overachiever?

You don't have to look far into his past to understand his pain. As the child of David and Bathsheba, Solomon was born in scandal. The gossip columnists must have had a field day at the news of his birth.

And even the sappiest soap opera would have a hard time competing with Solomon's story. He watched his brother Absalom try to kill their father in an effort to take the throne. And Solomon himself was forced to kill one of his other brothers in order to claim his place as king. His early years were filled with chaos and crime and hate and lust, and every other human failing you can imagine. His pain had to be overwhelming.

By the time Solomon took his throne, he was most likely a deeply wounded and dysfunctional young man. So he set out to overcome the scandal of his life through wealth and achievement. His reign as king of Israel became nothing more than an effort to erase his past and prove his worth to others. Yet for all his trying, for all his accomplishments, for all his efforts to overcome, his success brought only more pain.

In Solomon's words, "Nothing was gained under the sun."

Like Solomon, many of us try to deal with our pain through unhealthy ambition. We become workaholics, always striving for more. We tell ourselves, "If I can only meet that next goal, get that big promotion, take my business to the next level, buy the house I've always wanted, publish my first novel—then I'll be truly happy." But that day comes, and still we're left feeling void and empty. The pain is still there. So we set even loftier goals in our ongoing effort for relief.

I've witnessed countless people try to deal with their pain through unhealthy ambition, and it never works. The ghosts always come back to haunt us.

The Third Method: *We Meditate*

The third way many people deal with pain is to constantly focus on it. They become so hyperaware of their pain that they can't seem to think about anything else. I label these types of people "meditators," because they often allow their pain to become an all-consuming obsession. Their mind lingers over and ponders their pain in an unrelenting fashion—they meditate on it. Their misery is always in the front of their minds, and it seems to find its way into every conversation they have.

You may have been in a small group Bible study with a meditator. Many of us have, and it can become a pretty exhausting experience. Every study seems to become an avenue for them to vent and "explore" their struggles. They remember every bad thing that has ever happened to them, every event that has ever gone wrong in their lives, and they're quick to share their pain with anyone willing to listen.

I've known many meditators in my life, and I feel deeply sorry for them because they tend to alienate every friend they have. In an effort to deal with their pain, they constantly talk it through. Yet they never find a way to let go of their past and move forward. For all their conversing and processing, they never seem to find healing for their misery. All they accomplish is keeping the pain fresh and the scab reopened.

Absalom was a textbook meditator.

When Absalom learned that his brother Amnon had raped his sister Tamar, he didn't do anything about it. And neither did David, their father. Absalom simply allowed his anger to stew. He took his sister to live with him, and for two years he seethed in silence. Until one day he saw an opportunity to have his brother Amnon killed.

When David found out about Amnon's death, Absalom fled to a far country and spent three years in exile, hiding from his father and his other brothers. Eventually David sent for him and brought him back home, but their relationship was never the same. Absalom never forgave his father for overlooking his sister's rape at the hands of Amnon, so he continued to plot and scheme. Absalom did all he could to undermine his father's authority, and he did it by conspiring and talking behind his father's back. Eventually he was able to turn the Israelites against King David. And once that was accomplished, he began plotting to kill his father and take the throne.

Absalom was deeply wounded at a young age, and he never attempted to work through his pain. He instead used his pain as justification to harm others. Instead of allowing God to heal his wounds, he meditated on his pain, which only served to keep the wounds fresh.

Like most meditators, Absalom wasn't really interested in moving forward. It's almost as if he found a strange kind of comfort in misery. Meditators hang on to every injustice they've suffered, because they find more pleasure in bitterness than they do in consolation. They eventually develop a victim mentality and often become negative, cynical, and unforgiving.

Meditators are deeply unhappy people, and they're far more common than you might think. And the church seems to attract more than its fair share of them. I'm not sure why, only that they tend to gravitate toward places where it's acceptable to talk openly about their pain. I guess when the bars are all full they look for the nearest church.

We're All Wounded

Some medicate their way out of pain, others become unhealthy motivators in order to distract from their pain, while still others meditate their way through life in an attempt to justify their pain. We all deal with pain in some way, whether right or wrong, and we can all recognize ourselves to some degree within these three coping mechanisms. We all hurt, and we all seek relief from our hurts.

Obviously, not all of us are textbook cases of dysfunction. And most of us probably use a combination of these three coping mechanisms to get by.

When you hear of someone who is a "mean drunk," you can usually assume he is both a medicator and a meditator. He medicates his way out of the pain, then attempts to justify his behavior through anger and hostility.

A woman who goes through a bitter divorce might try to overcome her insecurities by becoming a workaholic. She becomes an unhealthy motivator. She vows to never again let herself become poor and vulnerable, so she turns into an overachiever, constantly striving for success and financial security. She may also spend much of her time meditating on her pain, sabotaging her ex-husband's relationship with their kids. She tries to build herself up by tearing him down and is never quite able to let go of her pain and bitterness and move forward.

We are all in some way victims to the wounds we've experienced. And we all have different ways to try to salve the pain. But we will never find true healing until we stop struggling to overcome our pain on our own and instead give our wounded hearts to God.

Accept God's Blessing

Jesus said, "Blessed are those who mourn, for they will be comforted" (Matt. 5:4).

Jesus wasn't saying that sadness is a blessing, because we all know that isn't true. It hurts to mourn. It's painful to mourn. It's excruciating to be so wounded that our only response is to weep and grieve. Mourning for the sake of mourning is not a blessing.

What Jesus was saying is, "When life gets hard, bring your pain to me and I will comfort you." The blessing is that we have a Savior to lean on in times of pain. We have a place to go to find healing. We have a God who loves us deeply enough to wipe away every tear.

The blessing is that we have a friend who can—and will—bring supernatural healing to even the most devastating and scarring wounds that have hidden deep within the hurt pocket of our spirits.

There is no wound that God cannot heal. There is no pain that he cannot remove. There is no sorrow so deep that he cannot resolve it.

But first we have to let him in. We have to find the strength to open our hands and our hearts and surrender our pain to God. We have to let him inside the deepest, darkest, most wounded regions of our spirits. And that's not an easy thing to do.

I know how hard it can be to open up and let God bring healing. For years I struggled with this issue. I was so deeply hurt and wounded that I completely shut myself off from the world. The feelings of rejection and injustice I experienced as a young boy were devastating, and they created within me a staggering level of insecurity and doubt.

Those years when I acted out in rebellion were some of the most painful years of my life. I created a tough exterior, but inside I was dying. My anger was nothing more than a way to keep my pain hidden from others. And the pain very nearly destroyed my spirit altogether.

During the early years of our marriage, Karen used to say to me, "Jimmy, you don't know how wounded you are. You don't know how devastated you are by the things that happened to you as a boy."

And each time she said that I would deny it. I would straighten my shoulders, stiffen my jaw, and say, "I'm not hurt. It wasn't that big of a deal."

I refused to acknowledge the pain. I couldn't bring myself to admit how much it hurt. And because of it, the wounds I carried inside very nearly destroyed every relationship I ever had, including my relationship with Karen.

The pain also made it impossible for me to build a meaningful relationship with God. And that was perhaps the greatest tragedy of all.

My first step toward freedom came the day I finally found the strength to drop to my knees and acknowledge the depth of my pain. When I was finally able to open up to God and say, "I really hurt."

Healing came only when I was able to ask God for help. When I finally overcame my prideful spirit and said to Jesus, "I'm in such pain, Lord. I need your blessing."

Jesus has the desire and the power to heal. But before he does that, you and I have to take the first step.

If you've never acknowledged your pain to God, I encourage you to do that today. If you've never owned the depth of your sorrow, there is no better time than the present.

Give God access to the deepest, most painful parts of your heart so that healing can finally begin. Let God do for you what he has done for so many others. Because the pain we hide from God becomes Satan's greatest tool for chaos and destruction. The wounds we try to bury give the devil an unrestricted foothold in our hearts and lives. And once he has that kind of access, he can create even greater pain and misery.

Takeaway

- People often believe that "time heals all wounds," but that's not true. Time often makes pain grow even worse.

- Unprocessed pain has to be dealt with. And left to our own devices, most of us will always deal with it in the wrong way.

- Only God can bring true healing to our hearts and help us resolve the unprocessed pain residing in the hurt pocket of our spirits. But that healing can only begin when we decide to give him access to the deepest and most painful areas of our hearts.

PART 2

The
Hurt Whisperer

Your enemy the devil prowls around like a roaring lion looking for someone to devour.

—1 Peter 5:8

There is no truth in him. When he lies, he speaks his native language, for he is a liar and the father of lies.

—John 8:44

—5—

The Message in the Pain

God whispers to us in our pleasures, speaks in our consciences, but shouts in our pains.

—*C. S. Lewis*

The Dr. Phil Show once featured the story of a young woman who seemed to have everything going for her. She was a world-class athlete who had won seven Olympic medals, including two gold. She was a beautiful girl who had successfully parlayed her Olympic celebrity into a lucrative modeling career. She had everything so many of us strive for: fame, fortune, success, and beauty. And she was barely twenty-five years old.

For all practical purposes, she should have been the happiest, most content person on the planet. But she was miserable. Inside, she was eaten up with pain and self-doubt.

She could hardly contain her tears as she described her overwhelming sense of worthlessness and shame. For much of her life, she had suffered crippling feelings of low self-esteem and self-hate. She attempted to overcome her pain through drugs and alcohol, and even developed a dangerous eating disorder. Eventually she began cutting herself, and she once cut her arms so badly that she likely would have bled to death had a fashion photographer not found her on the bathroom floor.

On the outside this young woman seemed to have it all together, but on the inside she was dying.

The Message of Pain

It's impossible to tell by looking at a person what pain lies beneath the surface. Often those who appear to have life by the tail are the ones who hurt the most. I'm always astonished to learn what pain is hiding inside the hearts of the seemingly happiest and most successful people.

In the case of that deeply wounded young athlete, her struggles began at the age of twelve when her parents divorced. Like most children of divorce, she internalized the blame for her parents' breakup. She began wondering what she had done wrong. It was during this time that she threw herself into sports and developed a deep need to excel at every sport she played.

She became a classic motivator, trying to salve her pain through ambition and success. Her need to achieve drove her to become the best in the world at her sport, but even that couldn't take away the pain.

"Everything I did was an attempt to get the attention of the two people I loved the most," she said through her tears.

Unprocessed pain is a dangerous and deadly force. It can cripple and debilitate even the strongest spirit. But the pain itself is not the real culprit. The true enemy is the message within the pain. Our real internal struggle is with the damaging lies we allow our wounds to whisper into the depths of our hearts.

The message in the pain leaves us most wounded.

When parents divorce, the message in the pain can be an overwhelming burden for an insecure young child to bear. The pain whispers to them, "This is your fault. You caused this to happen. If you were a better person, your parents would have stayed together."

When an insecure junior high boy feels victimized by his schoolteachers and principals, it isn't the pain or rejection that causes him to rebel. It is the message within the pain. The pain whispers to him, "Nobody cares about you. No one cares what happens to you. They just don't want you around."

Pain, at its core, is not necessarily a bad thing. Pain can cause us to grow and reevaluate. God often uses pain to discipline us and to redirect the course of our lives. Pain in itself is usually a tool for learning and reexamination.

But the damaging whispers we hear in the midst of pain are never from God, and they are never healthy. Those messages are always from the enemy. And they are always chock-full of lies.

When Satan Speaks

Satan speaks to us through our pain because pain is often a place of darkness and confusion. Pain has a way of catching us off-guard and unaware. And the more we hurt—the more unresolved pain we harbor within our hurt pocket—the more vulnerable we are to the enemy's lies of deceit.

As a young boy, I developed a lot of insecurities, and most of them revolved around the way I looked. I was an extremely big kid for my age. In the second grade I was the tallest kid in my class, even taller than the teacher. And because of my height, I often hunched when I walked.

I also had a huge silver tooth in the front of my mouth. I had lost that tooth when my neighbor shot a rock from a slingshot at me, and in those days silver was cheaper than porcelain. So the dentist fixed it by putting a shiny silver tooth right in the front of my mouth.

My brothers called me "Bucky the Silver-toothed Beaver." I'm not sure which one came up with that nickname, but they both thought it was hilarious, so it just stuck. I always laughed with them when they called me that, but inside it hurt deeply. I felt like a freak of nature.

Every time I looked in the mirror, all I saw was this giant kid with a big ugly gopher grin. And my second-grade class picture confirmed what I had always imagined others saw when they looked at me.

I'll never forget the day those photos came back from the printer. Every other kid in class had this sweet picture of themselves with per-fectly combed hair and a cute angelic smile, like you'd see in a Sears catalog.

And then came my picture. I looked like the hunchback of Notre Dame, with my enormous body and that horrible silver grin. Like someone had taken the grill off an old Buick and attached it to the front of my face. The kids had a good laugh at my expense that day, and it hurt far more than I could ever allow anyone to know.

The pain of feeling so ugly and different was devastating to me. But it was the message in the pain that hurt the worst. I thought to myself, *No wonder they make fun of me. I'm a freak. I'm a disappointment to everyone. How could anyone ever love me?*

Messages of pain guided me through much of my early years. I always struggled to feel worthy—or even normal. Throughout my grade school years I felt different from the other kids, and I was convinced that everyone else thought the same thing about me. I felt rejected by others, and though I knew my parents loved me, I always feared that if they ever saw the real me they would be deeply disappointed.

Even during the early years of our marriage, these insecurities haunted me. As an adult, I had long since gotten rid of that awful silver tooth, and most of my peers had caught up with me in size. I no longer stood out as a freak, but inside I still felt like one. The feelings of doubt and uncertainty were imbedded so deeply within my spirit that they never let go. No matter how much I tried to shake them and tell myself that those days were in the past, the feelings of shame and worthlessness still remained.

Satan continued to use the pain of my early years against me. He never stopped whispering lies of ugliness and rejection into my spirit.

Lies from the Enemy

I'm not the only one Satan lies to.

Karen is one of the most beautiful women I've ever known. She was beautiful at the age of sixteen when we first met, and she still is. And she's never had a problem with her weight. Yet at an early age she suffered deep feelings of insecurity and self-loathing. People who know her today have a hard time believing that she ever had such feelings, because she really is a stunning woman. Yet she never felt pretty.

During the first few years of our courtship and marriage, I knew that she was quiet and reserved, and I often wondered why she was so shy. I had always assumed that she was just an introvert who didn't enjoy being the center of attention. But I quickly learned how wounded and fearful she was. Inside she was terrified of letting her guard down around others.

Once she was able to discuss her insecurities with me, she confided feelings that I never imagined she had ever experienced. She told me she had always felt stupid and abnormal. Even though she was a good student, she was convinced that something was wrong with her mentally. And she felt fat and unattractive, even though others always told her how beautiful she was.

She also told me how sinful and unloving she'd always felt, and couldn't imagine that God could forgive her. This confession left me completely baffled, since Karen is the godliest, most morally upright person I've ever known. She's never stolen so much as a paper clip, and I think her lips would explode if she ever uttered a curse word. But somehow she got the message that God was displeased with her.

All these thoughts stayed with her throughout her childhood years and even into adulthood. Because of that, insecurity and doubt became the guiding force of her life.

Something in Karen's past set her on a path toward fear and self-hatred, and that wasn't an accident. Satan saw the wounds from her youth and began using them to tear her down. He began whispering thoughts of sin and ugliness and unworthiness into the depths of her spirit. And like most of us, Karen began to believe the enemy's lies.

Today Karen is a completely different person. With God's help, she has successfully overcome those feelings of fear and self-doubt. She is a bold and confident spokeswoman for God, and I'm continually amazed at her wisdom as she comes to life during the taping of our *Marriage Today* television program. You would never know today that she ever struggled with feelings of insecurity. But that's only because she allowed God to heal her heart and renew her mind.

When God Speaks

If it weren't for pain and tragedy, Satan would have a lot of free time to sit on his hands and sulk. Oh, I'm sure he'd still be busy, because Satan also uses good times to deceive us. But he'd certainly have to work a lot harder. Tragedy can give Satan a powerful foothold in our lives. It's during times of pain and vulnerability that he can do the most damage.

But it's also during such times that God can do the most good.

Just as Satan uses tragedy to tear us away from God, God uses tragedy to draw us nearer. It's the ultimate two-edged sword. Pain can easily alienate us from God, but it can also make us lean on God even more.

One of my favorite Bible passages is found in 1 Kings. The prophet Elijah was desperately seeking a word from the Lord, so God told him, "Go out and stand on the mountain in the presence of the LORD, for the LORD is about to pass by" (1 Kings 19:11).

So Elijah went to the mountain and stood in the cleft of a rock to wait for God.

> Then a great and powerful wind tore the mountains apart and shattered the rocks before the LORD, but the LORD was not in the wind. After the wind there was an earthquake, but the LORD was not in the earthquake. After the earthquake came a fire, but the LORD was not in the fire. And after the fire came a gentle whisper. (vv. 11–12)

I love that God spoke to Elijah in the form of a "gentle whisper." And he often speaks to us that way today. I've experienced it a number of times, and you likely have too.

But Elijah knew that God doesn't always speak in a whisper. Sometimes he speaks to us through the whirlwind. Other times he speaks through the earthquake. Still other times he speaks to us through the fire. Throughout Scripture we often see God speaking through times of turmoil and chaos. And that is still true today.

God speaks to us through pain because it's often during times of pain that we realize how much we need God.

I'd rather hear God's voice come to me in a gentle whisper, but I don't always listen for his voice as I should when the world is quiet.

It sometimes takes pain and tragedy to get me to seek God on certain issues.

How to Tell the Difference

So if God speaks through pain and the devil speaks through pain, how can we know for sure who is speaking?

When God speaks, it is always to build us up, never to tear us down. God is in the business of hope and restoration. When his voice comes, it always comes to guide and comfort, even when it is a word of rebuke or correction. He moves us toward growth and character and holiness. He encourages us to see ourselves through his eyes, as sons and daughters of the King.

God's voice is the voice of love and grace and forgiveness. It is never the voice of fear and doubt.

In contrast, Satan's voice brings nothing but fear and doubt. He comes to us in the form of insecurity and self-hate. His voice is one of confusion and uncertainty. Satan comes to convince us that we're ugly and stupid and sinful, that we're not worthy of God's love and goodness.

Satan's voice is the voice of hopelessness and despair.

Most of the messages we hear through our pain have nothing to do with God. Those damaging inner voices I heard as a boy were nothing more than lies from the pit of hell. The voices that whispered into the depths of my spirit, "You're a freak. You're ugly. No wonder they don't like you." These accusations were intended to rip me out of God's hands, and they very nearly succeeded. I thank God that he continued to pursue me and woo me toward his love, even during some of my darkest days.

The voices that spoke to Karen's spirit, trying to convince her that she was stupid and ugly and unworthy of God's forgiveness, were nothing more than the enemy's attempt to break her tender spirit. But it didn't work. I thank God every day that he brought healing to Karen's heart.

And the damaging messages you hear in the midst of chaos are just as untrue. The voices that say to you from the depth of your pain, "You're no good. You're a disappointment. You can't change. You'll never be smart enough, pretty enough, loving enough, genuine enough, worthy enough for God's forgiveness." These are not the voices you need to acknowledge or believe.

The voices that try to convince you that you'll always be different, always be hopeless, always be unlovable, always be in pain, that you'll never be happy, never get to heaven . . . those are the voices you need to silence. Those are the voices you need to shun. Those are the chains of bondage that need to be broken.

And only God can help you break them.

The Gentle Whisper

Jesus said, "The thief comes only to steal and kill and destroy; I have come that they may have life, and have it to the full" (John 10:10).

The devil has evil plans for your life, and you don't need to listen to anything he has to say. He is an evil and vindictive liar whose eternal fate has already been sealed. He only speaks because misery loves company, and there's no creature on earth more miserable than the devil.

But God's voice brings life and joy and happiness. With God's voice comes hope and restoration. God can heal the painful wounds of your past and renew your wounded heart.

Your job is to discern which voices are speaking and to learn how to respond when they do. To turn a deaf ear toward Satan and listen instead for God's gentle whisper.

_____ *Takeaway*_____

- Unprocessed pain is a dangerous force that can cripple even the strongest spirit. But it's the message in the pain that does the most damage.

- Satan is the father of lies, and he uses painful moments to try to tear us down and separate us from God. I call Satan the "Hurt Whisperer" because he stealthily speaks lies into our spirits during times of pain.

- These deceitful messages bring pain and insecurity into our lives and often work to isolate us from God.

- God also uses times of pain to speak into our spirits and draw us nearer. God speaks through pain because often it is painful times that remind us how much we need him.

–6–

Whispers of the Enemy

The first step on the way to victory is to recognize the enemy.

—*Corrie ten Boom*

I'm convinced that Satan's greatest strength is his subtlety. He knows how to stay under the radar.

If the devil came to us the way we often imagine him, with crooked horns and a rusty pitchfork, dressed in fire-engine red from head to toe, I don't know many people who would listen to him. But that's not how he operates. Satan is cunning and shrewd and stealthy. Scripture tells us he often "masquerades as an angel of light" (2 Cor. 11:14).

And he comes to us primarily when life feels dark and dreadful. Satan is called the "prince of darkness" for a reason. Anytime something painful or damaging happens in our lives, he is there to whisper thoughts of hopelessness into our spirits. He will say anything to keep us from the purposes that God has created us to accomplish.

Wherever you find rejection, abuse, disappointment, failure, sin, sickness, trauma, and suffering, you can bet that Satan is right there, waiting to capitalize on it.

I call Satan the "Hurt Whisperer," because that is the most common way in which he works. You'll never hear the devil shouting his vile plans from the rooftop, because he knows how counterproductive that would be. He prefers to hide in the shadows and work under the cover of night.

And that's what makes his voice so dangerous and deadly. He doesn't present himself as he is, but as he wants us to see him.

How Satan Speaks

There are two specific ways that Satan speaks to us in order to conceal his identity. Two perfect disguises that the enemy uses to tear us down and keep us confused.

First, he comes in the form of a simple inner thought—as if the words came from our own hearts and minds. He embeds negative feelings and ideas within us and tries to convince us that they are just harmless inner emotions.

When a young boy gets a poor grade in algebra, or struggles to get through a history test, he may think to himself, "I'm just so stupid." He thinks the thought is his own, and it could be. But when it becomes chronic and begins to encompass his life, you can be sure it's a whisper from the enemy.

When a middle-aged woman looks in the mirror and sees age lines forming at the corners of her eyes, she may think to herself, "When did I get so old? I'm so ugly! No one will find me attractive." But those thoughts are not from within. They are assaults from the enemy.

When a young boy or girl is sexually, verbally, or physically abused, you would think they would be able to understand that they are innocent victims and didn't deserve it. But in almost every case they begin to say to themselves, "Something is wrong with me. It's my fault. I deserved this."

Many times the thoughts inside are not our own. They are implanted by the enemy to make sure the damaging event turns into a devastated life.

Second, Satan comes masquerading as God. He implants damaging and harmful ideas that he wants us to believe come from above, but they are only lies from hell.

On the heels of sin, you and I often think to ourselves, "I'm such an idiot. I'm just a worthless sinner. I'm not worthy of God's love."

It may feel like a bout of conviction coming from the Holy Spirit, but it's not from God. Such thoughts are nothing more than a lie from the enemy's mouth. They come in the form of a whisper disguised as God's chastising voice, but they are the enemy's words, meant to drag us down and damage our relationship with Jesus.

In his second letter to the Corinthian church, Paul warned believers not to be deceived by such lies from the enemy. He writes, "I am jealous for you with a godly jealousy. I promised you to one husband, to Christ, so that I might present you as a pure virgin to him. But I am afraid that just as Eve was deceived by the serpent's cunning, your minds may somehow be led astray from your sincere and pure devotion to Christ" (2 Cor. 11:2–3).

Paul begins the passage by reminding the Christians at Corinth of their true identity in Christ. They are the perfect bride of Jesus. They are a people set aside for greatness in God's kingdom. And then he warns them not to be deceived by the enemy into believing anything less.

Eve was created for God's purposes, and she was a perfect bride for Adam. She was flawless and unblemished before God, and she knew her Creator's voice, yet she was still deceived by Satan's cunning.

Paul was warning the Christians at Corinth, "Don't underestimate the devil's ability to deceive you. He is far more skillful and crafty than you might be led to believe."

Paul understood how Satan works. He knew how sly and deceptive the devil could be. And he knew how quickly the enemy's lies could get into the hearts and minds of God's people, keeping them from embracing their true identity in Christ and even destroying their relationship with God altogether.

A Voice in the Garden

When Satan came to Eve in the garden, he came in the form of a serpent. Eve trusted the serpent; she had no reason not to. All of God's creations lived in harmony in the Garden of Eden, so it was a perfect disguise on the part of the devil.

And the first thing Satan did was to question God's words. "Did God really say, 'You must not eat from any tree in the garden'?" (Gen. 3:1).

It's no accident that the first recorded utterance from Satan in the Bible begins with Satan questioning the words of God. Because that's where the devil always begins. Satan can't implant his own thoughts in our minds until he first causes us to question God's thoughts. The two ideas cannot coexist.

It's impossible to believe your identity as God's most beloved creation and still accept the identity that Satan needs to instill within you. He has to first convince you to reject what you know in your heart to be true.

Satan knows he has to disarm you before he can defeat you.

And isn't that the way he still works today?

The reason Satan uses times of pain to speak into our lives is because pain often leaves us feeling vulnerable and confused. The Bible tells us that God loves us, that he has a wonderful plan and purpose for our lives. But in the midst of pain it's easy to question those words. Satan comes to us and whispers into the depths of our spirits, "Does God really love you? If he does, why did he let this happen? And where is he now?"

Satan uses pain to catch us off-guard. To make us feel alone and abandoned.

And no pain is more primed and ready for Satan's words of deception than aged and unprocessed pain—the kind of pain that builds and grows inside the hurt pocket deep within our spirits. That's where Satan finds the kind of wounds and sores that make his job easy. That's where he finds a breeding ground for emotional confusion and doubt. That's where he knows he can do the most damage.

When we stuff unprocessed pain into the darkness of our hurt pocket, it remains fresh and untended. Inner wounds don't heal themselves, they simply remain exposed and defenseless. The wounds we try to hide and shield from further pain only grow and accumulate, causing even greater pain and misery.

And wherever you find a hurt pocket brimming with pain, you'll find Satan questioning God's goodness, twisting God's words, confusing God's purpose, whispering lies of deceit and destruction into our hearts.

"Did God really say that?" he whispers. "Does God really care about you?"

The enemy disarms us in order to defeat us. And it's sad how often his tactics work.

Naked and Ashamed

Once Satan convinced Eve to question God, getting her to eat the fruit was a small hurdle. Anytime you find someone confused about God's word, sin is inevitable. It's the obvious next step.

And sin always feels less sinful when we have company, so Eve convinced Adam to eat the fruit as well.

Scripture records, "Then the eyes of both of them were opened, and they realized they were naked; so they sewed fig leaves together and made coverings for themselves" (Gen. 3:7).

What's the first thing you and I do when we sin? We try to hide our sin from God. We try to cover up what we've done. We cower in shame, because anytime we fall for Satan's lies, shame is the response he's after. He shames us into sin, and then shames us for sinning.

He begins by coaxing us into disobedience. "What are you, a coward? Are you really afraid of eating a small piece of fruit?"

Then, once the deed is done, he wags his bony finger in our direction. "Look what you've done now! God is never going to forgive you for that!"

The irony would be laughable if it weren't so deadly and destructive. And effective.

So Adam and Eve hid when they heard God walking in the garden.

The Lord called out to Adam, and Adam answered, "I heard you in the garden, and I was afraid because I was naked; so I hid" (v. 10).

God's response to Adam was probably not the response he expected. "Who told you that you were naked?" (v. 11).

God was saying to Adam, "You didn't hear that from me. Who's been whispering in your ear? Do you think I'm shocked by your nakedness? I created you that way."

God wanted Adam and Eve to know that they had been listening to the wrong voice. That they had been deceived into thinking that God was ashamed of them.

And you and I need to hear that same message.

God is not shocked by our nakedness. He understands our frailties and vulnerabilities. He understands our pain. He understands the humanity that causes us to sin, and he loves us in spite of it. You and I were created in love, and no amount of sin can destroy that love.

It isn't our nakedness that drives us away from God; it's our hiding. It isn't sin that keeps us distant; it's how we respond on the heels of sin. It isn't God's voice speaking shame into our hearts; it's the voice of the enemy.

Hiding from Shame

Adam and Eve had a perfect life, and they had a perfect relationship with God. They were created in God's image, and he placed them in the garden where they all lived together in harmony. It was exactly the way God designed it to be, and Satan hated every minute of it. He hated seeing Adam and Eve in such a right relationship with God and each other. He hated that Adam and Eve were so happy and content and unburdened by sin. He despised everything about their existence.

Satan hates you and me as well, and he hates any type of healthy relationship we enter into. He hates marriage and families and anything that brings purpose and fulfillment into our lives. And he especially hates the relationship we have with God. So he tries to destroy it.

Satan's ultimate goal is to separate us from God, because any life apart from God is a miserable and lonely existence. And he does that through lies and deception. He coaxes us to sin, because sin brings shame. Then he whispers into our spirits, "Look what you've done! Look how naked you are! God will never love you now!"

Satan knows that shame makes us pull away from God, makes us recoil from his presence, causes us to hide in the shadows of the garden.

But God isn't fazed by our nakedness. God isn't shocked by our sin. God says to us, "Who told you that you were naked? Who told you I was angry? Who told you I don't love you anymore?"

God can handle our transgressions. It's our hiding and pulling away that makes him seem so distant. It's when we believe the enemy's lies that shame and embarrassment come into our hearts and lives. And those things never come from God.

God's voice brings only forgiveness and restoration. God seeks us out when we hide. He pursues us in the midst of our sin, and he says to us, "Who told you that you were worthless? Who told you I couldn't use you? Who told you I wouldn't forgive you? Who told you I couldn't love you?"

Every one of us, at some point in our lives, in the midst of pain and confusion and disobedience, will hear the enemy's voice whispering lies into the depths of our spirits. And it's so easy to believe those lies. It's so easy to feel shame. And shame always makes us want to hide and cower.

But God says to us, "Don't hide from me. Don't distance yourself from my love. Let's deal with your sin and move forward."

When Satan Interprets

Like Adam and Eve, the apostle Peter also found himself faced with confusing messages from the enemy. And he was just as quick to believe the words.

For three years, Peter had walked with Jesus as his disciple. He saw Jesus perform countless miracles. He watched firsthand as Jesus healed the sick, brought sight to the blind, made lame men walk, even raised the dead back to life. There was no doubt in his mind that Jesus was the Messiah. That he was God come in the flesh. Peter knew Jesus's voice well.

But still he found himself deceived. Here's how Matthew records the story:

From that time on Jesus began to explain to his disciples that he must go to Jerusalem and suffer many things at the hands of the elders, the chief priests and the teachers of the law, and that he must be killed and on the third day be raised to life. (Matt. 16:21)

Jesus took great pains to prepare Peter and the other disciples for what was to come. For three years he had walked with them, taught them, mentored them in the truth of God's Word. He had taken common fishermen and turned them into firsthand witnesses of God's power and authority over evil. He knew that these twelve men would be the carriers of God's message of salvation to all nations of the earth, so he taught them well.

But he also knew how hard it was going to be on them to see him crucified on a cross, and he didn't want there to be any confusion in their minds when that happened. So he told them what to expect.

But Peter had been listening to a different voice in his spirit.

"Peter took him aside and began to rebuke him. 'Never, Lord!' he said. 'This shall never happen to you!'" (v. 22).

Peter had just been given the best news he'd ever heard, yet he couldn't receive it. He couldn't imagine that this was God's plan.

Jesus was saying to him, "Peter, I'm about to perform a miracle to end all miracles. I'm about to bring healing and restoration to the world, once and for all. I have to die for the sins of mankind, but don't worry, Peter. In three days I'll be resurrected, and then everything will be different. Death will be defeated for good!"

Peter had been given a front-row seat to history's most pivotal event. Once Jesus completed his mission, the world would never again be the same. And Peter was about to be transformed into the most powerful man on the face of the earth. He would become the "rock" upon which Jesus would build his church. He was destined to become the preeminent apostle for God's church throughout the entire world.

Peter was hearing good news! But he couldn't see it that way, because Satan had already been speaking to his spirit.

And the enemy's voice had said to him, "You're just a fisherman, Peter. Nobody knows who you are. You came from obscurity and you'll go back to obscurity when Jesus is gone. Everything you've witnessed for the last three years will be forgotten. Jesus is going to die, and then you'll be left completely alone."

Peter couldn't hear the words of Jesus through the negative voices already entrenched in his spirit. So Jesus rebuked him.

> Jesus turned and said to Peter, "Get behind me, Satan! You are a stumbling block to me; you do not have in mind the concerns of God, but merely human concerns." (v. 23)

Jesus knew that Peter wasn't the devil. And it wasn't Peter whom Jesus was rebuking. It was a man under the influence of the devil. A man who had forgotten which voice to heed and which one to ignore. A man who knew God's voice well and should have known better.

God was speaking to Peter, and the devil was right there by his side interpreting the words. Satan's goal was to keep Peter from fulfilling his purpose and accepting the destiny that God had in store for him. He saw the fear in Peter's heart and used it against him.

How often does he do the same with you and me?

Married to the Devil

Anytime God speaks, Satan is quick to interpret. He'd like to interpret every event that happens to us, and that's exactly what he'll do if we let him.

In fact, I'm convinced that nearly every human conflict is the result of Satan's twisted interpretation of the facts. That's true in any human relationship, and especially in marriage.

I've been counseling couples for over thirty years, and I've seen a lot of miscommunication during that time. Most of it I attribute directly to the enemy's voice working through unresolved hurts from the past.

So often I will find myself in my office counseling a couple on the brink of divorce. I see these two sweet people in front of me, weary and deflated, emotionally worn out from the constant arguing. Usually they are people without a mean bone in their bodies.

Years earlier they fell in love and got married because they couldn't imagine being apart. Back then they used to cherish the time they had together and do nice things for each other. They would spend their evenings whispering sweet nothings into each other's ears. They would hold hands as they walked in the park and smile at each other across crowded rooms. And neither would think of uttering a harsh word about the other.

Now, years later, here they sit across the desk from me, arms folded over their chests, angry scowls on their faces, not even looking in each other's direction.

Both are convinced that they've somehow married the devil—or his ex-wife.

She begins telling stories of a cold and uncaring husband who takes her for granted, who doesn't care about her feelings, who hates her mother, who is distant from their children, who has no idea how to make her feel loved.

His turn comes and he tells of a woman who doesn't respect him, who is cold in the bedroom and hostile in the kitchen, who doesn't understand him, tries to control him, gives him day-old donuts for breakfast just to let him know she's angry.

She's convinced he is the Antichrist, and he's calculated the letters in her name and come up with "666."

And how did that happen? I'm sitting there with the task of untangling years of anger and resentment and rage, and each time I think to myself, "Why did they let things go this far? Why did they let their love die such a horrible death?"

In just about every case, what I'm witnessing are two good and decent people who have spent years letting Satan interpret the words and events in their lives. Somewhere along the way they stopped listening to God and each other, and began believing the voice of the enemy instead.

Aged Anger

"'In your anger do not sin': Do not let the sun go down while you are still angry," Paul warned the Ephesians (Eph. 4:26).

Anger is not necessarily a bad thing. God often uses anger to mobilize us to change. Righteous anger has caused people to do things they otherwise might have never done, like join a mission team to an impoverished country, go back to school and become a preacher, finally confront a brother steeped in sin, or run for political office.

Righteous anger is what Jesus had when he turned over the tables in the temple. Anger in itself is not a sin.

But aged anger is a different thing entirely. Aged anger is when we allow our rage to grow and fester. Aged anger is nothing more than human wrath, and wrath is reserved for God alone.

James tells us, "Everyone should be quick to listen, slow to speak and slow to become angry, because human anger does not produce the righteousness that God desires" (James 1:19–20).

I used to say that aged anger gives Satan a foothold in our lives, but it's much more than that. It's not just a foothold; it's an invitation. Like a big brass ring of resentment just dangling in the devil's face, daring him to grab hold and hang on for the ride!

That's why Paul warns us to settle our anger before the sun goes down, because aged anger is a dangerous and deadly thing. Aged anger is what you get after the devil has had the chance to work it over, to mold and shape our emotions into something they were never intended to become, to claw and scratch at the surface of the wound until it bleeds outrage and resentment.

Aged anger is what I see every time a couple sits in my office, both weary and frustrated from the constant battle, struggling to understand what happened to their once-happy marriage. One hundred percent of the time, what they are experiencing is the end result of letting Satan interpret the words and events of their life together.

Instead of listening to each other or to God, they believed the lies of the enemy.

Choosing the Voice You Hear

The same voice that spoke to Eve in the garden, twisting God's words and confusing her mind, speaks to you in the midst of your pain. When the world feels dark and dreadful, when crisis comes, when things happen that don't make sense, the enemy whispers in the depths of your spirit, "Does God really care about you? If he does, why did he allow this to happen?"

The voice that spoke to Peter's spirit as Jesus relayed his future, the voice that interpreted God's words before they ever reached Peter's ears, is the same voice that speaks to you and to me in the midst of confusion and chaos.

When the enemy whispers, all too often you and I are quick to listen. That's because we usually don't recognize that it's the enemy's voice speaking to us. We haven't taken the time to challenge the negative voices and hold them up against the light of what God tells us is true.

God tells us, "Nothing can separate you from my love" (see Rom. 8:39).

But the voices tell us, "God will never forgive you for that."

God tells us, "Come to me when you feel burdened, and I'll give you rest" (see Matt. 11:28).

But the voices tell us, "You're all on your own. No one cares what happens to you."

God tells us, "I will never leave you nor forsake you" (see Heb. 13:4).

But the voices whisper, "Where is God when you hurt? Where is God when you need him most?"

It isn't our pain that separates us from God; it's the voices we hear in the midst of our pain. And God won't heal the wounds until we start squelching and ignoring those negative voices when they come.

At any given time, you and I have two voices whispering into our spirits. One is a still, small voice, beckoning us to trust the truth of God's Word. A voice calling us to lean on God in times of trouble, to let him in when we feel lonely and alone, to give him access to the pain in our hearts and let him begin the healing process.

And then there's the whisper of the enemy, telling us to ignore God's Word, to stuff our pain and keep it hidden, to question the goodness of God.

Which voice we choose to heed is completely up to us. And it's the most critical decision we have to make.

When the devil's thoughts become your thoughts, they will eventually compromise everything about you. His lies will infiltrate every area of your life and every relationship you try to build. They will sabotage your relationship with your spouse, your kids, even your friends and acquaintances. And they will keep you from ever having a right relationship with God.

Takeaway

- Satan's greatest strength is his subtlety. Often when he speaks to our spirits, he speaks in the form of a seemingly innocent inner thought. Other times he comes disguised as God's voice.

- Satan knows that he has to disarm us before he can defeat us. When he went to Eve in the Garden of Eden, he coaxed her into sin by causing her to question God's goodness. He often uses that same strategy with you and me.

- God's voice always brings messages of love and grace and forgiveness. Satan's voice always brings messages of doubt and insecurity. It's important that we learn to tell the difference.

—7—

Clothed in Shame

There is no deeper wound than humiliation.

—*Irwin Katsof*

There's nothing more painful when you're young than watching your parents struggle. I remember a lot of tough times in my youth, but I honestly can't recall anything quite as agonizing as seeing my parents fight to keep food on the table. I'm sure we weren't the poorest family in the world, but we were a million miles from rich.

I had a roof over my head and three meals a day, but that's about all my parents were able to give me. I had to work for anything else I wanted or needed, so beginning at the age of ten, I took any job I could find.

My first job was a paper route. I'd get up at four every morning and deliver the morning newspapers on my bike. I actually kind of enjoyed it, and I especially liked having a little money jingling in my pocket at school.

I also sold donuts door-to-door. I'm not sure you could get away with that today, but at the time people loved opening their door in the morning to the smell of fresh donuts on their porch.

When I got older I started mowing lawns around the neighborhood. That was probably my favorite job, because I could make more in one day than I did in a week of throwing papers.

In the summers I would help local farmers work their fields. I'd do anything they needed done, from driving the plow to stacking hay in the barns. It was hot and grueling work, but it was steady. There was always something that needed to be done, so most days I'd work from dawn until dusk.

Later I got a job at the Scrub-a-Dub car wash, making about $1.60 an hour.

For a time I worked in the local feed house, but that didn't last long. It's a good thing, because I'm not sure my lungs would have survived more than a few months.

When I was in college, I started delivering appliances for my uncle's store.

From an early age I knew that if I wanted something I'd have to work to get it, because my mom and dad were tapped out.

The Burden of Poverty

At the time my two older brothers were attending school at Texas Tech University, and back then there weren't a lot of college loans to be had. Most kids were on the pay-as-you-go plan, which meant parents had to sacrifice a lot to put them through. That was the case with my family.

My father made a modest income as the manager of a furniture and appliance business, and suddenly he had two boys who needed a college education.

So often I remember hearing my dad on the phone with one of my brothers. They'd be laughing and joking about some funny thing that happened at school, then suddenly the conversation would turn serious. My brother would bring up a school bill that needed to be paid or another book he needed to buy, and my dad would start rubbing his forehead with his fingers.

I'm sure my brother felt bad about bringing it up, but my dad would do his best to reassure him. "I'll take care of that as soon as I can," he'd say. "Just give me a couple of days to come up with the money." He'd try to sound calm and relaxed, but you could almost feel the stress in his voice.

I knew how tight money was at home, and I never wanted to be a burden to my mom or dad, so I learned early not to ask for things I didn't need. Sometime around junior high, when I started my first job, I began paying all the expenses I could in order to help my parents out.

Through those years, I learned a lot of good lessons about working hard and being responsible with money. It's good for kids to work and to be productive. Kids need to learn the value of a day's wages. I made sure my kids were raised with those same values.

But I also grew up with a lot of unhealthy mind-sets—one in particular that has stayed with me throughout my adult life. Because money was tight and my parents were so financially stressed, I always felt like a burden to them. Anytime I needed something, I never wanted to ask, no matter how important it was, because I knew they couldn't afford it. So I just stopped asking. I'd simply work harder so I could take care of my needs on my own.

A lot of kids grow up poor, and not all of them feel the way I did. I'm still not sure why I was affected so deeply by my family's financial struggles. But the message I got was very real and profoundly painful. I felt like a burden to my parents, and those thoughts never quite let go of me.

First Real Job

My first good-paying job after I got married to Karen was selling appliances in a local store. It wasn't my dad's store, but one of his competitors. I started out in the warehouse, delivering stoves and refrigerators, then soon worked my way up to salesman. I got to wear a tie and everything. Just like a real grown-up.

Salesmen worked on a commission basis, and I knew I'd be good at dealing with customers.

My boss said he would pay me 6 percent commission on anything I sold, so I hit the floor running my first day on the job. Even I was surprised at how good a salesman I turned out to be. I was a natural and got even better with each passing day. There were days when I couldn't ring customers up fast enough. I'd have three sales going all at the same time, and customers waiting in the wings behind them. And every time I made a sale, I'd keep a running total of my commissions in my head. I was never good at math, but I could sure count money.

At the end of the month, Karen and I sat down at the kitchen table and added up my first commission check. When we finished, Karen's jaw dropped to the floor. It was going to be $3,200! In just one month! The previous year I had only made about $7,000, so this was more than we ever imagined I'd make. We spent all evening dreaming of the things we were going to buy. We even had our dream house in Beverly Hills all picked out and just waiting for us to move in.

I woke up bright and early the next morning and put on my favorite tie, then whistled all the way to work. I couldn't wait to collect my money. I was standing by the counter when my boss walked over and handed me my paycheck. I looked down at it, did a quick double take, and immediately my smile faded. The check was for $1,500.

I said to my boss, "Didn't you promise to pay me 6 percent commission?"

He said, "I know I said that, but if I paid you that much you'd be making more than my top salesman. And I just can't do that to him."

I took a short step back and looked at my check again. I wanted to say to him, "Actually, I think I am your top salesman!" But those words never reached my lips. I just stood there staring, feeling stunned and deflated.

Later that day he called me into his office to tell me he had restructured my commission agreement. He lowered my commission so that I couldn't make as much as the guys who had been there longer. I didn't say anything at the time, but it was a deeply painful and humiliating experience. And I dreaded going home to Karen and explaining why my check had been cut.

I guessed Beverly Hills would have to wait.

Driven by Guilt

What my boss did was incredibly unfair. It was a monumental insult, and it hurt me deeply. Yet for some reason the emotion I felt most was guilt. Like it was somehow my fault. Once again I felt like a burden.

All those negative feelings I had as a child began to resurface. I actually felt guilty for selling so much. I felt guilty for outselling the other salesmen on the floor and for putting undue stress on my boss. I even felt guilty for taking the check for $1,500.

It was clear that my boss had taken advantage of me, yet I placed the blame completely on myself. That didn't make sense in any universe, but somehow that's how my mind translated it.

Even after that humiliating experience, I worked hard to sell appliances for the store. And every month when payday rolled around, I'd feel guilty when I got my check. Even though I knew I was making less than those around me, I didn't feel worthy of my boss's money.

At the time, I didn't understand these conflicted emotions. I had never processed my inner thoughts enough to know the source of my feelings of shame. I just had no sense of self-worth, and I didn't understand why.

These feelings of guilt had become the guiding thoughts of my life, not only as a child but well into my adult years. I never felt like I deserved anything I got. And I could never ask for anything I wanted from others.

These insecurities also made me a terrible husband to Karen. At an early age I learned to keep my emotions hidden, to stuff them deep inside and never let them out. I never wanted to talk about my feelings. When I got hurt, I'd clam up and keep the anger hidden. I never wanted to burden anyone with my problems, so instead I bottled them up and kept them to myself.

My need to be self-dependent very nearly destroyed my marriage. Inside I was wounded and insecure and vulnerable. But on the outside I was determined to look strong and self-confident. I could never let anyone see the pain I felt inside.

Haunted by Shame

Years later, when God called me to be a pastor, I took a job with Trinity Fellowship Church. At the time it was a big cut in pay for us, but I wanted to be obedient to God's calling, so I committed to making it work. We had to make a lot of sacrifices in order to live on less.

But even then I felt like a burden. The church was small and struggling at the time, and I didn't want to take anything away from the other ministries. I even paid for church supplies out of my own pocket. If I needed a box of pens or a notebook to prepare my sermons, I'd pay for it with a personal check. And I still felt guilty every time I got paid.

I would work twice as long as anyone expected, often arriving at the office early, then staying after everyone else had gone home. I had a deep need to prove that I was worth what the church paid me.

I justified it by telling myself I was being a good steward of the Lord's money, but I've since come to realize that I was simply driven by this strange sense of inner guilt. I hated the thought of being dependent on others. I couldn't stand the idea of being a financial burden on the hardworking members of our church.

When a member would ask me to perform a wedding or a funeral, or officiate at some other function outside of church hours, I couldn't make myself charge a fee. I always felt like I should do these things for free.

And later, when the church began to grow, I started getting offers to speak at other churches and weekend seminars out of town. Even then I felt bad about charging. I would usually tell them, "I'll let you decide what you can afford to pay." Often they would take up a "love offering" after I spoke, and that would usually cover my expenses.

Despite my dysfunctional mind-set, the Lord always took care of us, and for that I'm grateful. I had never been able to shake those damaging and irrational thoughts I had developed as a child. I was convinced that I was nothing more than a burden on those around me, and the shame of that inner message still haunted me.

A Message from God

Through the years, God would often bring conviction to my spirit about this negative attitude. I knew it was wrong of me to be so self-dependent. It was actually based more in pride than humility, and pride is always a sin. But I never quite understood the depth of my shame in this area.

Then one day years ago, during my morning quiet time, an incredible event occurred. I was reading the Bible and meditating on God's Word. I silently prayed, "Lord, if there is anything in me that you want to deal with, please let me know. I'm listening, Lord."

At that moment God spoke into my spirit. It wasn't an audible voice, but it was very clear.

The Holy Spirit said to me, "You are not a burden; you are a blessing." It was as clear a message from God as I had ever received.

At that very moment, something pierced into my innermost being, something real and palpable, a sensation that even today, all these years later, I have trouble explaining or comprehending. I felt an instant sense of inner healing in my spirit.

And when that happened a flood of emotions welled up inside of me. All those painful memories of my childhood came to the surface. All the ways I had been keeping my pain and insecurity hidden from those around me. All the ways I had wounded Karen and others through my deep-seated need to be self-sufficient. All the ways I had tried to ignore the pain and keep my inner wounds hidden from God.

Until that moment I had never quite understood the depth of my pain or the source of my wounds, but God revealed those things to me. And for the first time in my life I felt completely free from the guilt and shame. I understood the miracle God was performing in my heart, and I no longer felt like a burden!

I've felt God's healing touch in my heart before, but often that healing has been gradual. He usually works on me over a period of time. But this miracle was instantaneous. I was completely free of all those negative thoughts and emotions. The messages of guilt and shame that had silently guided my life for over forty-five years were suddenly gone. And they have never returned!

Through New Eyes

Seeing yourself as you are, instead of who you've always projected yourself to be, is an unnerving experience.

I had never imagined myself as someone who was driven by pain and guided by pride and insecurity. I never knew how much my past had affected the way I viewed myself and those around me. I never realized how much it had affected my relationship with God.

When you feel like you're a burden to God, you're incapable of truly seeing him as the loving and generous Father that he is. You don't take your needs and desires to him the way you should. You don't embrace your inheritance as a child of the King.

You begin to feel more like a servant than a son.

Before that time I had spent years preaching and teaching on the goodness of God, and I believed it with every fiber of my being. But until that moment I had never been able to truly embrace that teaching. Suddenly I began to understand God's grace on an entirely different level.

Layer upon layer of scales began to peel from my eyes, and I was able to see God more clearly than I ever had before. I no longer felt like the runt at the end of the litter. I knew I deserved every good gift that God wanted me to have. I belong at the banquet table. I am a cherished child of the King!

And so are you!

We All Struggle

I have a belief that is as unshakable as any spiritual conviction I've ever had: I believe that there are no accidents in God's economy. I believe that God directs the details of our lives and that everything happens for a reason.

Because I believe that, I'm convinced that if you have found yourself on this page, God has brought you here for a reason. That is no accident.

God wants you to know that you are not a burden to him. That your struggles are not hidden from his eyes. That your feelings of fear and shame and insecurity did not originate with him. That your sins are not too great for him to handle. That your wounded spirit is not damaged beyond his ability to heal.

God knows the pain you've experienced and the damaging thoughts that have silently guided your life. He understands your struggles, and he's waiting to set you free.

Maybe you struggle with a spirit of poverty. You've worked hard all of your life, doing everything you possibly can in order to provide for your family, yet you still can't seem to make ends meet. No matter how many hours you work, or how many times you try to change jobs or careers, you never seem to get ahead. The bills pile up and the financial responsibilities continue to grow, and every month you fall farther and farther behind.

You tell yourself, "I just wasn't meant to succeed. I guess I'm destined to be poor."

Or maybe you struggle with trust. Somewhere in your past you were let down by people who were supposed to have your back. Someone who should have taken care of you instead turned their back and left you to fend for yourself. Maybe your father left you at a young age, or your mother was emotionally distant. Maybe your best friends at school abandoned you. Perhaps you have a string of painful memories that haunt your thoughts. Everyone you ever trusted somehow let you down, so now you keep people at a distance. You keep yourself safe by pushing others away. You want to trust, but you can't seem to break through the insecurities and fears of the past.

You say to yourself, "I just can't let people in. They will always let me down."

And because of it, you struggle to trust God as well. You've given your life to him, but you have always held back a small piece of your heart.

Perhaps you struggle with forgiveness. You confessed your sins when you first came to Jesus, and your remorse was genuine. You truly wanted to believe that God could forgive you for your past, but in your heart you've always wondered. A small piece of you has always held back, never quite accepting that you are truly forgiven. You've never quite grasped that God could overlook the things you've done, not to mention the things you continue to do.

You think, "I'm such a sinner. There's no way I'll ever be truly forgiven."

Maybe your battle is with failure. Years ago God put a mission on your heart and you've struggled ever since to accomplish it. You know that God has a purpose for your life, and you long to see him fulfill that purpose through you. Yet time and again you see nothing but setbacks and failures. Things never seem to work out as planned. You've convinced yourself that God will never be able to use you. And many of your prayers are riddled with thoughts of guilt and shame and failure.

You pray, "Lord, why can't I do anything right? Why do I always disappoint you?"

The Problem of Shame

When thoughts of fear and shame guide our lives, we will always struggle to feel loved and accepted by God. And we'll never be able to build truly deep and meaningful relationships with others.

Our marriages will suffer. Our careers will falter. Our goals will fall flat. Our emotions will run high and our wounds will remain deep. Our feelings of failure and insecurity will always keep us from accepting the good and perfect things that God has in store for us.

God longs to free you of these damaging inner messages. He is waiting to do a miracle in your heart and life. And the first step toward freedom is to acknowledge your chains and to recognize who put them there in the first place.

God is not the author of your shame. It didn't originate with him. It is the enemy of your soul who used the pain and experiences of your past to put you in bondage to fear. Satan is the one who took your accumulated wounds and turned them into a mountain of shame and doubt. The devil's lies are what put thoughts of worthlessness and abandonment in your spirit.

And only God can unshackle you for good. Only through God can you find ultimate release from the enemy's chains.

So many of my early experiences in life made me feel like a burden to others. But there was one particular experience I had that didn't fit that mold. It was something that happened during my early twenties, and it has stuck in the forefront of my memory ever since. Looking back, I can see that God orchestrated this gift to me as a foreshadowing of his love.

He gave me this memory and then kept it fresh for a reason.

A Gift from God

It happened just a couple years after I had quit my job as an appliance salesman and had gone to work with my dad in his appliance store. He took on a partner to help us grow the business. I had always dreamed of what I could do with my dad's business if he let me help, and now I had my chance to show him.

My dad couldn't pay me much, but I didn't mind. I was more interested in helping him succeed. I'd spent much of my childhood watching my parents struggle, and now I was intent on helping him get ahead. So I worked harder and longer hours than I'd ever worked.

I slaved away at the store, overseeing the warehouse and making sure the showroom floor was filled with product. Every time we sold an appliance I made sure it was delivered on time and installed with care. I tended to all my customers as if they were my new best friends. I threw myself into the job so that the business would grow and prosper.

And I never once asked for a raise. Even when sales were at an all-time high, I was content with what I made. I just loved seeing my dad so happy.

Then one day, after I'd been working with my dad for about two years and right after the holiday season, my dad came to me out of the blue and handed me a check for a thousand dollars.

"What's this for?" I asked him.

"I just wanted to thank you for all your hard work," he said.

I didn't expect it and tried to give it back, but he insisted that I take it. He told me he appreciated everything I had done for him and wanted to bless me, even if it was just a small blessing.

That check might as well have been for a million dollars, because that's how much it meant to me. Just knowing how much he loved and appreciated me was worth more than all the money in the world.

People will often say "It's the thought that counts" when you give them a gift, but they don't always mean it. In this case, I can honestly say it was the thought that meant the most to me. And I'll never forget the glint in my dad's eye as he handed me the check.

I could tell it was a special moment for him as well.

But that isn't even the best part of the story!

A few days later I was working in the warehouse and my dad was minding the front counter when a car pulled into the parking lot. It was the financial partner my dad had taken on several years earlier.

Apparently he had just found out about the bonus my dad gave me, because he stormed in the front door, and without even saying hello he bellowed, "What do you think you're doing giving your son a bonus like that? What did he do that's so special? You know we can't afford to be giving money away like that!"

I crept up closer to my dad's office so I could hear better, but not so close that they could see me. I didn't want them to know I was listening. My dad wasn't saying a word, just letting his partner vent. I began wondering if I was going to have to give the bonus back.

There was a long pause, and then suddenly I heard my dad speak.

"Don't ever tell me how to run this business," he said. "If you want me to buy you out, I'll do it. And if you want to buy me out, we'll talk about that too. But don't ever come in here and tell me that I can't reward my son for all the work he's done! Do you know how much he's helped this store? Have you seen how hard he works? He deserves that bonus. Don't ever come in here again and tell me I can't bless my kids!"

I had never heard my dad so angry, and his response took me back a bit. But after the initial shock, it was his words that resonated in my spirit. I couldn't believe he stood up for me that way. It meant so much to me that he would come to my defense the way he did. His words touched me far more than he could possibly have known.

For so many years I had felt like a burden to my family, and to hear my dad call me a blessing was a gift too powerful for words. It was all I could do to keep from bursting out in tears.

You Are a Blessing!

Though I didn't see it at the time, I'm convinced that God arranged this event in order to speak into my spirit. He was saying to me, "Pay attention to this, Jimmy! I'm trying to teach you something here. You are not a burden to your father. You are not a burden to those around you. And you are not a burden to me!"

God wanted me to know that I was a blessing, not a curse. That I was loved, not despised.

God wanted me to know that I was worthy of the good things he desired to give me.

You and I spend so much time wrapped up in thoughts of fear and doubt and shame that we seldom stop to ask God what he thinks of us. We're so busy nursing our own insecurities that we forget to take time to listen as God speaks into our spirits.

We say to God, "I don't deserve to be called your child. I'm such a failure. I'm so sinful and useless. I know you could never use someone like me."

And all the while God is shaking his head, thinking, *Haven't you even been listening to me? Haven't I told you how much I love you? I sent my Son to die for you. Why are you still listening to the enemy's lies?*

It's amazing to me that a God who's never broken a promise could be so doubted, while a devil who's never kept a promise could be so trusted.

If God were to speak to your spirit at this moment, I know exactly what he would say to you. He would say, "Who told you that you were naked? Who put those negative thoughts in your head? You didn't hear that from me."

You are not a disappointment to God. You are not a failure. You are not useless to him. You are the beloved child of the King of the universe! You deserve all the good things he has in store for you. You deserve to be happy. You deserve to be healed. You belong at the banquet table!

You are not a burden to him. You are a blessing!

Takeaway

- As a young boy, I dealt with a lot of shame and insecurity because of my parents' financial struggles. And these feelings affected my life well into adulthood.

- When thoughts of fear and shame guide our lives, we will always struggle to feel loved and accepted by God. And we will never be able to build a truly meaningful relationship with him.

- Because of my early experiences in life, I always felt like I was a burden to God. But God taught me that I am not a burden to him; I am a blessing. God wants you to internalize that same truth.

—8—

Thoughts Held Captive

Whatever is true, whatever is noble, whatever is right, whatever is pure, whatever is lovely, whatever is admirable—if anything is excellent or praiseworthy—think about such things.

—*Philippians 4:8*

Writing a book is a lot like riding a roller coaster. It always feels like a good idea before you get started, but once you're in the middle of it, you wonder what you've gotten yourself into.

It's definitely therapeutic, since it forces you to process your thoughts and challenge many of your long-held assumptions. What you put on paper needs to stand the scrutiny of time, so it's important to test your theories well before you put them in print.

But it also has a way of bringing a lot of painful memories and experiences to the surface, many of which you thought you had buried for good. That's especially true when you're writing a book on pain.

The thought has occurred to me that if you've read this far and haven't read any of my previous books, you probably assume that I had a horrible childhood. You might even be lighting candles for me, wondering how I ever survived it.

But that's not the case. I had great parents and a lot of wonderful experiences as a boy. I actually had a pretty normal childhood. I had a doting mother, a caring father, brothers who looked out for me, and a number of great friends in the neighborhood.

Like many of us, however, I did experience a lot of pain in my youth, and it's usually the painful things we remember the most clearly or repress the most strongly. Negative and hurtful experiences often have the most profound effect on our lives and future.

It's amazing how good memories can fade so quickly, yet the bad ones stay with us well into our aging years.

And that is no accident. It is an enormous testament to the power of the enemy's tactics and the reality of his destructive work in our lives. I've learned to never underestimate the enemy and his ability to use our painful experiences against us.

A Simple Memory

Painful memories are not the only ones we remember, but they're often the ones that most define how we see ourselves. They also tend to define how we see God.

As I process the negative memories of my past, it becomes extremely clear to me why I struggled for so long to feel loved and accepted by others. I understand why I felt like a burden to those around me. The thoughts that silently guided my life and emotions were tied directly to those memories that proved to be the most painful. And they were all memories of shame and rejection.

Just fleshing out the material for this book brought back to the surface an event I hadn't thought about in years—a memory I didn't even realize remained in my subconscious mind.

It happened during the summer of my fifth-grade year. I played Little League baseball at the time, and it had always been the highlight of my summer. All my friends played on the team with me.

I loved baseball and played at every opportunity. Even when practice was over, my brothers and I would come home and play baseball in the street, usually long after dark. At the age of ten, baseball was the most important thing in my world. I couldn't get enough of it.

Then one day after practice I came home for supper and my mom said to me, "Jimmy, I hate to tell you this, but you can't play on your team anymore."

I was taken completely aback. "Why? What did I do?" I asked her, assuming I was being punished for something.

"You didn't do anything," she said. "But you just had your birthday, remember? You turned eleven last week, and the rules say you can't play past ten."

I stood with my mouth wide open. "But all my friends are on the team," I said.

"I'm sorry," she said, "but there's nothing I can do. Those are the rules."

That seemed completely unfair to me. *Why would they kick me off the team just because I had a birthday? I didn't do anything to them! Who makes up these stupid rules anyway?*

I knew it wasn't my mom's fault, but I blamed her nonetheless. I went to bed angry that night, and I sulked for the rest of the summer. All my friends got to finish out the season, and I had to sit on the sidelines and watch. In my mind, it was a tragedy of epic proportions.

How could they do this to me? What did I do wrong?

It's a simple, seemingly insignificant memory that shouldn't have left such an indelible mark on my young life. And if it were an isolated incident, it probably wouldn't have. But it was just one of many instances in my childhood that left me feeling victimized by those in authority over me. It felt like every time things were going well in my life, some authority figure would reach in and yank the rug out from under me.

Many of these stories I've already shared with you. Every time the school board would redraw the district lines, it felt like they were just looking for ways to tear me away from my friends. And when they weren't banishing me to a different district, they were making me quit football. I couldn't even flirt with a few cheerleaders without getting licks from the school principal.

And the message I got from these unfair experiences was a deeply hurtful one. I was convinced that anything good that ever came into my life would be taken away from me. I felt like I didn't deserve to have good things in my life. I felt like I was a burden and a bother to everyone around me.

This message wasn't true or valid, but it became the guiding thought of my life. It was the message that the Hurt Whisperer spoke into my spirit time and again.

My only real problem was that I believed him.

The Messages We Hear

I'm not good enough.
I'm not talented enough.
I'm not smart enough.
No one wants me around.
People can't be trusted.
I'll always be disappointed.
I'll always be poor.
God can never forgive me.
God will never love me.

These are but a few of the many lies Satan uses to tear us away from God and keep us from becoming the people God created us to be. He continually whispers these lies into our spirits until his thoughts become our thoughts. His goal is to keep us in shame, to keep us in doubt, to keep us fixated on our nakedness before God, to keep us hiding in the garden.

We will never be free from these crippling thoughts until we purposefully challenge them, holding up the devil's lies to the truth of God's Word, replacing Satan's thoughts with God's thoughts.

Paul wrote in his letter to the Ephesians, "For our struggle is not against flesh and blood, but against the rulers, against the authorities, against the powers of this dark world and against the spiritual forces of evil in the heavenly realms" (Eph. 6:12).

The damaging and demeaning messages you hear in the depths of your pain are not figments of your imagination. They are evidence of a very real battle going on in the spiritual realm. This is a battle between two kingdoms, and it is being played out every day in your heart and mind.

Every thought that crosses your mind comes from one of three sources. It is either God's thought, Satan's thought, or your thought.

And your thoughts almost always reflect the voice in your spirit you have been listening to the most.

When our minds are fixed primarily on God and his Word, God's voice has the greatest influence over our thoughts. When we think on pure and noble things, our thoughts are being guided by God.

But when our minds are fixed on earthly things, on our own wants and desires, on our own pain, our thoughts are almost always being guided by the enemy.

And what we think is critical, because our thoughts determine who we are and what we become. Proverbs 23:7 says, "For as he thinks within himself, so he is" (NASB).

Our lives are not just affected by our thoughts, they are *defined* by them. You become what you think you are.

I recently heard the story of two people, both of whom died of cancer. One was a man we'll call "Ryan," the other was a young woman we'll call "Rebecca."

Ryan and Rebecca had a lot of similarities. They were both believers, and both were about the age of fifty when cancer was first diagnosed. Both were from loving, Christian families. Ryan had four kids; Rebecca had three. And both died from their cancers at the age of fifty-five. But the ways they allowed their sickness to affect them were in stark contrast.

Rebecca's Story

When Rebecca first learned of her sickness, she turned to her church family for support. Every week friends would gather at her house for prayer. And each time, they began with an hour of Scripture reading and Bible study. She immersed herself in God's Word and would often read the Bible late into the evening hours.

Treatment was hard on her body, and though she went through several rounds of chemotherapy, nothing seemed to work. The cancer had spread too far. Her friends prayed for a miracle, and many were convinced that God would heal her. Rebecca believed that as well. But she was completely at peace with the thought of dying. Often she would say to her friends, "I know the Lord can heal me, but I won't be sad if he doesn't. I'll just get to see him sooner than I expected."

As the years inched by, her sickness only got worse. But she never lost faith. She continued to trust God with her future. Eventually she became bedridden and was transferred to a hospice for her last few months. She could no longer read on her own, so each time visitors came to see her she would ask them to read the Bible to her. She had marked her favorite passages with dog-ears and highlighters, and those were the ones she wanted to hear. Most were from the Psalms. She also asked friends to sing hymns to her, if they wouldn't be too embarrassed.

The day Rebecca died, her room was filled with friends from her church. Her pastor was there, as well as her children, and a few members of the church choir. They were singing her favorite hymn when she finally slipped away. It was a sad moment for everyone, but Rebecca was completely at peace. She died with a smile on her face, cradling her well-worn Bible across her chest.

It wasn't until after Rebecca's death that they realized how many people she had touched during her final few months on earth. While in hospice, she had witnessed to many of the nurses and patients on her floor. Three nurses and six patients had given their lives to Christ, and numerous others had recommitted themselves to the Lord. On the news of her death, people began flooding into her room from all corners of the hospital, each with a different story to tell about how their lives had been moved and changed by Rebecca's unshakable faith in God.

Ryan's Story

Ryan also died of cancer, and he was taken to hospice for his last few months, but his death was not nearly as peaceful. And his testimony wasn't one of faith, but of fear.

The moment Ryan learned of his cancer, he began outwardly blaming God. Though he had been a believer most of his life and even served as an elder in his church, he couldn't understand why God would let him get sick. He had so much left to do, and several of his kids were still living at home, so he pleaded with God to take away the disease and let him live. His friends would often meet at his house to pray for him, and each time Ryan would break down in tears of sorrow. "Why would God do this to me?" he would cry. "I've tried to be faithful! I've tried to do what God wanted me to do! I don't want to die!"

When the doctor told him that nothing more could be done, Ryan argued with him. "Are you telling me you're giving up?" he asked. "Surely there's some other type of treatment you could try?" He refused to believe that his life was over. He couldn't understand why God would take him at such a relatively young age.

Ryan's family took care of him at home as long as they could, but eventually the doctors encouraged them to move him into a hospice. While there, Ryan spent much of his time sulking, angry that his family had abandoned him. When they came to visit he would beg them to take him back home with them. Often his words would become hurtful, causing them to leave in tears.

The day Ryan finally passed on, he was surrounded by family and friends. And his death was anything but peaceful. As he felt his life slipping away, fear completely enveloped him.

One of his sons took him by the hand and tried to reassure him. "It's okay, Dad. Everything is going to be okay."

But Ryan lashed out at him. "No, it's not okay! Things are not going to be okay! You don't know the things I've done! God will never accept me! I don't want to go to hell!"

Ryan passed away that day with a look of horror in his eyes. His face was riddled with fear and shame and confusion. He took his last breath convinced that his soul was lost forever. Though he had trusted Jesus for salvation many years earlier, he had never truly embraced God's forgiveness. He had never accepted that grace could cover his deepest sins.

The Power of Our Thoughts

In my heart, I believe that both Ryan and Rebecca are safe today in the arms of Jesus. They both put their faith in Christ, and God promises to redeem us when we look to him for salvation, regardless of the depth of our sin.

But the contrasts surrounding their deaths bear witness to the power of our thoughts.

When Rebecca learned of her sickness, she responded by turning to God. Instead of hiding from God, she ran toward him. She sought him out and began filling her heart and mind with thoughts of praise and worship. She ignored the negative voices in her spirit and instead listened for the voice of God.

But Ryan took a different approach. His sickness caused him to lash out at God, to act out in fear and anger and rebellion. Instead of filling his mind with heavenly thoughts, he immersed himself in pity and doubt. He ran from God and tried to hide his nakedness in the garden. In the midst of pain and confusion, he tuned out God's voice and instead listened to the voice of the enemy.

Paul tells us, "Do not be anxious about anything, but in every situation, by prayer and petition, with thanksgiving, present your requests to God. And the peace of God, which transcends all understanding, will guard your hearts and your minds in Christ Jesus" (Phil. 4:6–7).

Any thought that leads to anxiety is not from God. Any thought that causes us to doubt God's love, to worry about the future, to fret over our past, to live in a state of confusion and fear, is always from the enemy. And it only happens when we allow the devil's thoughts to become our thoughts.

But God's voice leads to peace that transcends all human understanding. It silently guides us out of fear and doubt and brings only thoughts of trust. God's voice whispers messages of faith and hope and love. When our thoughts become God's thoughts we become a living testament to God's faithfulness, even in the midst of death.

The key, then, to triumphant living is to learn, in every circumstance, how to make God's thoughts our thoughts. Paul tells us, "We have the mind of Christ" (1 Cor. 2:16). If you are a believer who has put your faith in Jesus, then the mind of Christ is already living within you. He is already alive and active in your spirit, guiding, directing, correcting, speaking, whispering his thoughts into the depths of your heart. You just have to begin tuning your heart and spirit to his voice. You have to learn to recognize God's voice when you hear it, discerning the good and godly messages from the ones that mean only to do you harm.

But how exactly do we do that? How do we neutralize the enemy's voice in our spirits and overcome the negative thoughts when they arise? How do we disarm the devil and defuse his hold on our lives?

I believe we do it by remembering these three simple steps:

Expose the Enemy's Lies

Paul tells us, "Have nothing to do with the fruitless deeds of darkness, but rather expose them" (Eph. 5:11).

The first step in overcoming the enemy's lies is to expose them for what they are. It's impossible to fight an enemy without first recognizing that enemy when you see him. You have to know whom you're fighting against.

At any given time, I have a lot of conflicting thoughts that pop into my mind. And most of them have roots somewhere deep in my spirit. When temptation comes, it always comes from within.

There are a lot of things I'm not tempted to do. I've never been tempted to rob a bank. I could stand in line all day at the teller's window and never once think to myself, "I should try to take their money." I might be tempted to get angry if the line moves too slowly or if someone steps in front of me, but the devil would never whisper into my ear, "Why don't you rob them?" He knows that's not something I would ever do. And if I heard that whisper in my spirit, I would know it didn't come from me. The enemy would easily be exposed.

But there are things I am tempted to do that are almost always rooted somewhere in the pain of my past. When I am driving on the highway and a huge 18-wheeler cuts in front of me without yielding, I can easily be tempted to act out in rage. A voice deep in my spirit will rise up and whisper, "Who does he think he is? What an idiot! What gives him the right to cut me off like that?"

The voice comes because the temptation is a very real one for me. I've acted out in anger before, and I can easily be tempted to do it again.

When I'm at the grocery store patiently standing in line at the checkout, and suddenly the cashier turns off her light and closes her register, I can easily be tempted to say something rude and unkind. A voice from within tempts me to say to her, "Do you know how long we've been waiting in line? Are you seriously going to make us move over? What kind of store is this?"

I'm usually able to overcome that temptation and bite my tongue, but that wasn't always the case with me. There was a day when I would have told her off without giving it a second thought. And that's why the temptation is there. Because the possibility still resides within my spirit. The temptation is real because it is rooted in the pain of my past. If I sense that someone is taking advantage of me, all those times I was hurt and violated by those in authority over me come welling up to the surface. The enemy knows me well. He knows the pain of my past, and so he uses that knowledge against me.

It's my job to understand my pain, to recognize the voice of the enemy, to discern evil thoughts and expose them before they cause me to do harmful things.

Expel the Enemy's Voice

Paul wrote, "For though we live in the world, we do not wage war as the world does. The weapons we fight with are not the weapons of the world. On the contrary, they have divine power to demolish strongholds. We demolish arguments and every pretension that sets itself up against the knowledge of God, and we take captive every thought to make it obedient to Christ" (2 Cor. 10:3–5).

Once we recognize the voice of the enemy, our second response should be to take our evil thoughts captive. This means we are to *demolish the arguments* we hear the enemy whispering into our spirits and instead make our thoughts *obedient to Christ*.

To take something captive is not a passive concept. It's a violent and deliberate act. It's something you do when you're in the throes of war. The things you don't kill or destroy, you take into captivity. You make them your prisoner. You take the damaging and impure thoughts that come into your mind and put them in shackles.

You bind the enemy's thoughts and cast them out of your mind.

At first you may have to do that a thousand times a day. When I first committed to renewing my mind and casting out thoughts from the enemy, the only immediate change I noticed was that temptations began coming at me from all sides. The more determined I was to expel the enemy's voice, the more he spoke into my spirit. His attempts to bring me down increased exponentially. I went through a season of tremendous struggle and temptation. The more you try to bind the enemy, the angrier he becomes. It's a very real dynamic, and one that you are sure to experience once you make that same commitment.

But don't allow yourself to become discouraged or deterred.

"It is for freedom that Christ has set us free," writes Paul. "Stand firm, then, and do not let yourselves be burdened again by a yoke of slavery" (Gal. 5:1).

There is freedom to be found from the enemy's yoke, but only for those willing to stand firm in their convictions. There is freedom for those who refuse to give up. There is freedom for those who determine to take the enemy's voice captive and cast it out of their lives.

You and I are to demolish every argument that the enemy throws our way. Each time the devil whispers thoughts of anger or self-doubt or condemnation into our spirits, we are to take the thought captive and expel it from our minds. We throw it as far from our conscious thoughts as possible and rebuke the enemy's voice.

Express Agreement with God

Once we've exposed the enemy's lies, casting them far from our minds, we are then to fill that space with the truth of God's Word. We need to be aware of every thought, taking in those that are biblical and casting aside those that don't agree with truth.

Today I can say without shame or embarrassment, "I am not a freak! I am not a burden! I am not a disappointment to God! I belong at the banquet table because I am the King's son! I deserve every good thing God wants to give me! I am a beloved child of the Creator of the universe!"

I can say those things because I know them to be true. I no longer have doubt or reservation in my spirit. I no longer struggle with those feelings of insecurity and self-doubt that I once had, because I have cast those thoughts from my mind and chosen instead to come into full agreement with God. When God says something, he intends for it to be the final word on the subject. To question it is not only wrongheaded, it is a direct assault on God's authority.

Any thought or feeling that wells up in your spirit and contradicts what God says is true needs to be violently expelled. Thoughts of hopelessness and despair, thoughts of fear and doubt, thoughts of insecurity and self-deprivation, these thoughts are never from God. Cast them out. Demolish these arguments of the enemy and instead bring them under the authority of Jesus.

When Jesus said to Peter, "Get behind me, Satan!" he wasn't rejecting Peter; rather, he was disarming the arguments of the enemy. And you and I need to do the same thing when we hear the enemy's voice. We take his thoughts captive, cast them out of our hearts and minds, and replace them with God's thoughts.

And God's thoughts are readily found within the pages of Scripture.

You are fearfully and wonderfully made (Ps. 139:14). God loves you (John 3:16). God delights in you (Ps. 147:11). God rejoices over you (Isa. 62:5). The Holy Spirit dwells in you (Acts 2:38). You have the mind of Christ (1 Cor. 2:16). You are filled with all the fullness of God (Eph. 3:19). You are heirs to God's kingdom (Rom. 8:17). "You are a chosen people, a royal priesthood . . . God's special possession" (1 Pet. 2:9).

You are a blessing to him, not a burden!

These are the thoughts and words from God that you and I need to confess aloud and believe in the depths of our spirits. We need to say to the enemy, "I no longer accept your lies. I will no longer listen to your words of deception. I will no longer allow you to define my beliefs and actions!"

And then we actively bring our thoughts and speech into agreement with God and his Word. We permeate our speech with positive and uplifting words and begin filling our minds with Scripture.

Conquerors in Christ

So often you and I remain in bondage to negative thoughts and habits simply because we refuse to acknowledge the enemy's hold on our lives. We ignore the pain that resides deep within the hurt pocket of our spirits, never allowing God to deal with it and help us move forward. We see the devastation it brings to every area of our lives—to our marriages, to our friendships, to our sense of self, and to our relationship with God. Yet we never quite find the strength to confront these damaging and crippling lies that keep us in bondage.

We've allowed Satan a foothold in our lives, yet we've never found the courage and the tools to break free.

Those inner lies that Satan uses to keep you in bondage to sin and doubt are not who you are. They are not you. They are simply the thoughts that God needs to expel from your life in order to set you free.

If you struggle with an addiction to pornography, pornography is not your problem. Your problem is the thoughts that have held you captive to sin. Satan has convinced you that you are just a worthless sinner, that you are addicted to lust, that pornography is the only relief you'll find from the pain and fears that haunt you, that you are too weak and dependent to break free. The enemy keeps you in bondage through thoughts of shame and nakedness and by preventing you from embracing the freedom that is yours through Jesus.

If you are struggling with obesity, obesity is not your problem. If you struggle with alcohol, alcohol is not the issue. If you struggle with depression, depression is not your real enemy. Those struggles are symptoms of crippled thoughts that are holding you hostage. Your struggle is with the voice in your spirit that says to you, "No one cares for you. No one loves you. No one believes in you. You're too weak to break free."

And those thoughts are nothing more than lies from the pit of hell. They are lies that need to be exposed. Lies that need to be expelled. They are Satan's thoughts that need to be destroyed and replaced with God's thoughts.

And God says, "In all these things we are more than conquerors through him who loved us" (Rom. 8:37).

You and I have the power to conquer any lie the enemy whispers into our spirits, to destroy any damaging and negative thought that rises to the surface, to overcome any struggle that has kept us in bondage to sin. We have the power to break free from the Hurt Whisperer's chains of fear and sin.

We have a Hurt Redeemer—a God who can heal our broken hearts and set us free.

Takeaway

- Painful memories are not the only ones we remember, but they're often the ones that most define how we see ourselves. They also tend to define how we see God.

- We will never be free from the crippling thoughts that Satan whispers into our spirits until we start to challenge the enemy's lies and hold them up against what God tells us is true.

- There are three simple steps to expelling damaging and untrue thoughts about ourselves and God from our hearts: (1) we expose the enemy's lies; (2) we challenge and expel the enemy's voice when it comes; and (3) we express agreement with God's Word.

PART 3

The
Hurt Redeemer

He heals the brokenhearted and binds up their wounds.

—Psalm 147:3

Praise the Lord . . . who redeems your life from the pit and crowns you with love and compassion.

—Psalm 103:2, 4

—9—

Come Out of Hiding

> Among the many great things about admitting your weakness and vulnerability is that it is so relaxing. I don't have to be a fake anymore.
>
> —*Dan Hayes*

Mike (not his actual name) is the kind of guy most men enjoy being friends with. He's quick-witted and personable, has an awesome golf swing, understands cars and guns and football and all the other things guys like to talk about. He's a real "man's man" and fun to hang out with. He's also active in his church, and on the surface he seems to be a quality spiritual leader to his wife and two kids.

But I know things about Mike that not everyone knows. I know that behind closed doors, when no one is looking, Mike is an emotional bully to his wife and children. I know that Mike is a rage-aholic, who can be set off at the first sign of stress or confrontation from his family. I know that Mike is an addictive personality who struggles with pornography. He also has a problem with alcohol, though he professes not to drink, and you'd never find a drop of liquor in his cabinets. I know that sometimes, when his temper flares, his abuse becomes more than emotional. What Mike calls discipline, the rest of us would recognize as physical abuse.

I know that Mike's wife is in deep denial regarding her husband's problems. She spends much of her time keeping their family's secrets hidden from friends and acquaintances, especially people from church, and she has taught her kids to do the same. To outsiders she seems like the perfect Christian wife, caring and submissive, with a gentle and quiet spirit. But inside she is dying. And she dies a little more with each passing day.

Mike's friends from work and church would have a hard time believing what I know about him, because he seems so happy and normal. Just an ordinary guy with a house in the suburbs who keeps his lawn mowed, washes his car on the weekends, and waves to the neighbors as they pass by. You'd never pick him out of a crowd or think he had a care in the world.

And that is Mike's biggest problem. He keeps his true self hidden from the world around him. He keeps his addictions and his temper and his abuse swept under the rug. He would never allow his true character to be exposed. And if it ever were, he'd deny it to his very last breath.

I know some other secrets about Mike, but these probably won't surprise you. Though he comes across as a stable and happy person with a healthy self-image, inside he is a severely injured and insecure individual. In his spirit he is riddled with pain and anxiety. His mind is eaten up with thoughts of confusion and stress and self-doubt.

And his heart, no matter how hard he tries to hide or deny it, is profoundly and deeply wounded.

Hiding from God

Mike has been in hiding for so long that it has become second nature to him. He instinctively knows how to keep others from discovering the pain that resides deep below the surface of his heart. The wounds that have gathered in the hurt pocket of his spirit are so prolific and painful that they have kept him in a state of perpetual fear and isolation. He fears his secrets will be discovered, so he isolates himself emotionally, carefully keeping others, including his family, at a safe distance.

And the sad thing is, it doesn't have to be that way. Mike doesn't have to settle for such a sad and lonely existence. He doesn't have to hide. He doesn't need to live in pain and confusion. The wounds he harbors in his spirit could be healed, if only he could find the strength to come out of hiding and get help.

God can heal any wound, no matter how deep, no matter how painful, no matter how long it has been festering. He can change any heart, cure any addiction, and remove any unhealthy expressions of anger from our spirits. He can even reverse the chaos and damage created by abuse. God could heal Mike's broken heart and set him on a path to freedom, if only Mike would let him in.

"Therefore confess your sins to each other and pray for each other so that you may be healed," writes James (5:16).

There is healing to be found in the arms of Jesus, but it only begins when we find it within ourselves to take the necessary steps. We have to find the courage to ask for help.

We begin by confessing our sins to God. We come out of hiding, reveal our nakedness before the Creator, and ask him to forgive our rebellion. We acknowledge the gravity of our problem and the depth of our pain. And in the midst of our brokenness, we admit once and for all that we need healing.

Then we summon the courage to confess our sins and our pain to others. We find people we can trust, people who will pray for us, stand by us, walk with us on our journey toward healing. We find people who will hold us accountable.

Confession alone is not enough to bring healing. Mike has likely confessed his sins to God a thousand times, but once the brokenness lessens, he goes right back into hiding. The pain is still there. The wounds are still open and unprocessed. The rage and anger still simmer below the surface of his spirit.

If confession alone could heal a broken heart, Mike would have been healed years ago. But it takes more than that. God needs more than brokenness to bring healing; he needs our full cooperation. He needs us to come out of hiding, once and for all.

Immersed in Fear

I understand Mike's struggle far more than he might imagine. There was a time in my life when hiding was the only relief I found from the pain in my spirit.

Karen and I were only nineteen when we got married, and we both brought a lot of baggage into the relationship. Karen was deeply insecure, riddled with doubt about herself and her abilities. She was a beautiful young woman, but she never felt like it. The wounds of her past would never allow her to accept what a wonderful person she really was. Her defenses were constantly up.

And I certainly didn't do much to bring her out of it. I came into the marriage with a boatload of insecurities and anger issues. The unprocessed pain in my spirit had turned me into a deeply wounded—and wounding—individual. The inner vows I had made in my youth were still festering in my spirit. I had vowed that I would never again allow myself to be taken advantage of by others, that I would never again let myself be violated and wounded by someone who had authority over me. I was committed to always keeping the upper hand when dealing with others. I was not going to allow myself to be hurt again the way I was hurt so many times as a child.

That's a dangerous inner vow to bring into any relationship. But just imagine the damage it can do to a marriage.

I had given my life to Christ just a week before our wedding, and my conversion was real. My confession of faith was not a ruse or just a way to get Karen to marry me. I was sincere in my desire to live for Christ. But somehow I never fully surrendered the wounded part of my heart. I had given my life to Christ, but I had never given him my pain.

As a result, the first few years of our marriage were a living nightmare. I was an emotional brute before we married, but afterward I became a full-blown bully. Anytime Karen would come to me with a problem or concern, I would get angry and defensive. I would overpower her with words. I was good at arguing and never willing to admit when I was wrong.

And I never wanted to pray with her. Karen always wanted us to pray together, and she would bring it up every few days. But for some reason I just couldn't do it. I made a lot of lame excuses to Karen about why I would rather pray alone, but in truth, I was simply afraid of the intimacy and vulnerability it would bring. I couldn't allow myself to let my guard down that much. I was so afraid Karen would see the real me, and I just couldn't let her do that.

We had a lot of problems during the first years of our marriage, and Karen was intuitively dialed in to them. She knew we needed to learn to communicate better, so she would often ask me to sit down and talk with her about an issue. But I always refused. I was a hard-core chauvinist at the time, convinced that it was a man's job to take care of problems when they arose and a woman's job to sit back and let him do it. I really had no desire to communicate; I just wanted to talk, and I wanted her to listen.

That was probably my biggest shortcoming as a husband. I had come from a long line of rugged, prideful men who overcame adversity by pulling themselves up by their own bootstraps. We didn't need any help. We just needed others to get out of the way and let us do what needed to be done. We got through times of crisis the old-fashioned way: we gritted our teeth and plowed through it. I was the ultimate "lone wolf" male. Like Clint Eastwood, John Wayne, and Rambo, all rolled into one.

At least that's how I had always envisioned myself. In reality I was nothing more than a frightened little boy, hiding from the world, scared to death of getting hurt again.

Broken and Exposed

It's impossible to overstate the level of tension and dysfunction all of this created in our marriage. Looking back, I'm honestly surprised that

Karen stayed with me. If it weren't for God's supernatural intervention, we would have been divorced long ago. But God had a purpose for our lives and marriage, so he miraculously and graciously kept us together.

I knew we had a miserable marriage, and deep inside I knew that I was the real problem. But my pride never allowed me to own my role in the dysfunction. I was so afraid that if I ever let Karen win an argument or get the upper hand she would try to dominate me. And I simply couldn't allow myself to be overpowered. Especially by a woman half my size.

It was during this time that I developed a serious skin rash on my body. It wasn't an isolated rash but cropped up in several different places. I had no idea what it was, so I made an appointment with a dermatologist.

The doctor stripped me down to my shorts and did a thorough but quick examination, then put away his stethoscope and told me to get dressed. On his way out of the room he said, "The nurse will be back in a minute with some information for you."

I had no idea what he meant, but I put on my clothes and waited. A few minutes later the nurse came in and put a tape recorder on the table. "The doctor wants you to listen to this tape," she said. "Then you can check out."

Then she turned and walked out of the room.

I was stunned and began to get irritated. I had come hoping for some kind of prescription or medication, maybe a special soap or ointment I could use to clear up the rash. At the very least, I was expecting an impressive-sounding diagnosis for my disease. But apparently that's not what the doctor thought I needed. I couldn't imagine what good a stupid tape could do.

Until I listened to the recording.

It was an informational tape about the effects of stress and worry on the body, and the damage they can do when left unchecked. It explained how stress can actually cause physical sicknesses and disorders, like high blood pressure, hair loss, irritable bowel syndrome, and lower back pain. In many cases, it can even lead to skin disease and outbreaks of acne and rash.

As I sat listening to the recording, a flood of emotions welled up inside of me. I felt embarrassed that the doctor had seen through my tough exterior and diagnosed the true source of my problems. I felt helpless and exposed, knowing that he was probably in the next room writing down what he knew about me in my permanent medical file. I felt humiliated, thinking that the nurses were probably already whispering behind my back. And a big part of me was angry that I had been outed by the doctor. *Why couldn't he have just given me a salve and sent me home?*

But mostly, I just felt sad. Sad that I had let my marriage become so stressed and fractured that it actually caused physical strain on my body. Sad that I had allowed my pride and anger to bring such friction into our marriage. Sad that I had no idea what to do to fix the problem.

The tape finished, and I slowly gathered my things and made the long walk to my car in the parking lot. And then I sat in the car and cried. I couldn't remember the last time I had wept or even shown much outward emotion, but once I began to cry, the tears wouldn't stop flowing. The sorrow welled up so deep in my spirit that I could no longer control my emotions or gain composure. I saw people walking past me in the parking lot, and I was embarrassed that they could see me, but still I couldn't stop. I had never experienced such a deep well of grief and regret. I was completely undone.

I'm not sure how long I wept that day, only that it seemed like an eternity. And the entire time, I pleaded with God to forgive me. I begged him to take away the anger, to take away the stress, to take away the pride and arrogance and resentment. To remove my insecurities and my need to be in control. To stop my wounding tongue and biting words. To do whatever he needed to do in order to bring healing to our marriage.

I prayed for mercy and grace and restoration. And I prayed for supernatural strength as I committed to trying my best to become the husband that Karen needed me to be and the man that I desperately wanted to be.

The First Step toward Healing

My testimony would be so much more exciting if I could say that God brought immediate healing to our marriage that day. But that's not really what happened. What did happen was that God began a miraculous work in my heart.

The brokenness I experienced was a huge first step toward healing, and God was right there with me. But it was only the first of many steps I would have to take over the next few years. Karen and I still struggled to get along, and I still wrestled with the sin of pride. But little by little God began healing our marriage. He began dealing with my haughty spirit, revealing my flaws and insecurities, exposing the anger in my heart. With each passing day I could feel him working, refining, repairing, peeling off the layers of pain one by one.

Perhaps the most profound change that happened that day in the doctor's office was that I realized I had been exposed. It was the first time I could remember feeling so helpless and vulnerable and naked. My weakness had been uncovered. And I actually survived to tell about it.

It sounds bizarre to say it, even now as I write the words, but the most transforming part of the ordeal was that I knew I had been uncovered. Someone had peeked over the wall that I had so carefully built around my heart, and my world didn't implode. It actually was a freeing experience. I realized, probably for the first time in my life, that it was okay to be vulnerable. It was okay to let someone lift the veil and see my weaknesses. It was okay to expose the wounded spirit behind the mask. It was okay to hurt and to let others see my wounds.

It was a strange awakening. I was still insecure, still in hiding, still guarding my heart, but God was teaching me that it was possible to let others in and see the real me.

It was a simple lesson, but one that I needed desperately to learn.

A Step toward Hope

Karen and I still struggled in our marriage, and there were times over the next few years when I wondered if we would make it. We were still young and immature, and I had a lot of deep insecurities to work through. We would go through seasons of serenity and calmness when everything seemed to be going fine. Then suddenly something would happen and we'd be at each other's throats again. We'd stop talking for a few days, our anger would subside, and before long we'd forget what we were fighting about. Things would go back to normal.

It was almost as if someone had a switch that they flipped to control our relationship. They'd turn it on and we'd be fighting, turn it off and suddenly we'd be okay. It was an exasperating time in our marriage. And nothing was ever really resolved. Our differences would simply be moved to the back burner until the next time someone flipped the switch.

But some things were getting better. God had been working in my heart, and I honestly wanted to be a better husband. Each time we fought, a wave of conviction would flood into my spirit, and that's something I hadn't really experienced before. I was beginning to see more clearly the pain that I was inflicting on Karen and the damage I was doing by trying so desperately to stay in control. I had a deep desire to do better, and my prayers took on an even greater sense of remorse—and urgency.

I can look back today and identify a number of small turning points in our relationship during this time, but one in particular stands out in my mind. It was perhaps the most embarrassing but freeing experience of my life.

Karen and I had been getting to know an older couple at our church, Kerm and Lou Ethel Albertson. They taught the couple's class that we had been attending, and each week I found myself staying later after class just to talk with them. Karen and I never thought of them as mentors, but that's what they had become to us. They had the kind of marriage that we both longed to have. Kerm adored Lou Ethel and never had a harsh word to say about her. And Lou Ethel was crazy about her husband. I was envious of their relationship and often wondered what secret they had discovered.

Then one day Karen and I had another huge argument that seemed to go on for hours. As usual, neither of us seemed willing to back down. Eventually I got tired of fighting, threw up my hands in frustration, and went to another part of the house to sulk.

Later that afternoon Karen came into the room and told me to get dressed, because the Albertsons had asked us to meet them for dinner.

"When did you arrange that?" I asked her.

"Just now," she told me. "I called and told them we were fighting, and they asked us to go out for dinner."

I was furious. I couldn't believe Karen would do that to me. I couldn't believe she would share such intimate details of our lives with others, especially people I had been trying so hard to impress. I didn't want to go, but I knew if I didn't I'd be even more embarrassed. So I put on a clean shirt, feigned my best smile, and did my best to pretend everything was fine.

I can't remember the last time I felt as small and uncomfortable as I did that night sitting across the dinner table from Kerm and Lou Ethel, knowing that they knew we had been fighting. I hated the thought of others knowing our personal business. I had never been one to air my dirty laundry in public, and I wasn't about to start now.

But something happened that evening that changed everything for me. After dinner, as we were visiting over coffee and dessert, Kerm began to open up to us. He began telling us of the early days of their marriage and the struggles they went through as a young couple. They both laughed aloud as they recounted some of the silly arguments they'd had back then.

"Sometimes we'd go days without talking to each other," he said. "Then we'd start talking again and neither of us could remember why we started fighting."

He told us that there were times when they actually wondered if their marriage would survive. And the thought of that left me completely dumbfounded. I couldn't even imagine seeing them argue, much less fighting to the point of nearly destroying their marriage. I had always thought of them as the perfect couple, as "soul mates" who were born to be together. Suddenly I realized they were just like Karen and me!

That dinner had a profound effect on our relationship. Karen and I both went home with a renewed perspective. Though we didn't say it aloud, it was clear we were both thinking the same thing: *If they can make their marriage work after all they've been through, maybe there is hope for us, as well?*

Today Karen and I look back on that evening as one of the turning points in our marriage. We no longer saw ourselves as two stubborn people who should have never gotten married. In a strange way it made us feel almost normal. We knew that every couple had problems, but we had somehow convinced ourselves that ours were insurmountable. Suddenly we knew that wasn't the case. Knowing that the Albertsons had experienced the same kinds of struggles and yet came through them with a strong and happy marriage gave us renewed hope.

It was clear that God had arranged this dinner engagement. And we're so glad that he did.

The Power of Vulnerability

But there was another message I got from our evening with the Albertsons. This message was a bit subtler, but just as profound.

As I sat listening to Kerm talk about the many fights they'd had, even the intimate details of their arguments—all the times of stubbornness and disillusionment, the many times they had taken each other for granted, even times of pride and arrogance and sin—I was stunned that he could talk about his struggles with such honesty. He was completely unguarded and transparent with us, like an open book. He had nothing to hide. And the thought of that sent chills down my spine.

I could never imagine allowing myself to be that vulnerable. To let others see my flaws and insecurities. To be so embarrassingly honest. I couldn't imagine letting others see that far inside my heart and life.

And yet here was a man I respected deeply and admired as much as any man I had ever known, who had no problem sharing his deepest sins and inconsistencies with others.

God had been working in my life for several years to try to teach me the importance of opening up to others, but the lesson had never quite sunk in. In my mind I knew that it was wrong for me to be so emotionally closed and guarded. I knew it was wrong of me to keep my heart so protected, to be so defensive, to be so afraid of letting others in. But no matter how hard he tried to teach me, I couldn't make myself do it. I continued to guard my heart. I continued to be an emotional island.

I had never even opened up to Karen, much less other people.

But God used that experience to teach me the most profound and life-changing lesson of my life. Still today I consider it the most transforming concept I have ever learned.

In my heart I wanted to believe that the Albertsons' complete openness and honesty and vulnerability were just a few quirky traits they had developed after years of being together. I wanted to believe that they were just wired that way.

But God was teaching me otherwise. God was teaching me that those were the traits he used to save their marriage. That it was their willingness to open up and let others in that made their relationship so strong and vibrant. That their willingness to share their sins and struggles with others was actually the secret to their successful marriage.

Even more than that, it was the secret to their deep and meaningful relationship with God.

Called Out of Hiding

If brokenness alone were enough to heal our hearts, we would all be healed since each one of us has experienced moments of despair. We've all cried out to God in the depths of our pain for restoration or forgiveness or mercy. We've all been brought to a point of desperation and hopelessness and begged God for help.

But God needs more from us than brokenness. God needs us to come out of hiding. God needs us to confess our sins, to share our struggles with others, to do the hard thing and expose the chains that hold us hostage. God needs our willingness to be vulnerable and unprotected, to take off the many masks we wear in order to hide our flaws from others. God needs us to be held accountable, because accountability is a critical step in the healing process.

Today Karen and I have a phenomenal marriage. I honestly can't imagine living a day without her, and she feels the same about me.

We are closer than we ever imagined possible. There was a time when I couldn't even pray with Karen, but today we pray together regularly. It's the highlight of our lives together, and we jealously guard it. And we each have a relationship with God that is strong and vibrant and infinitely rewarding.

And the only reason any of that is true is because God called us out of hiding!

It's impossible to build a relationship with someone when your world is defined by fear, when you don't think you can trust them with your pain, when you try to keep others at arm's length. It's impossible to build a marriage without honesty and openness. It's impossible to feel truly close to another person when you spend most of your life trying to push them away.

The doubts and insecurities I harbored in my heart had crippled my ability to be a decent husband and father. And it wasn't until I finally came to the end of myself and started sharing my innermost thoughts and fears with Karen that God was able to step in and reverse the course of our marriage.

Once Karen and I learned to let our guard down and truly open up to each other emotionally, we began to see an immediate change in our relationship. The walls we had built between us suddenly started coming down, brick by sacred brick, and we began seeing things in each other that we hadn't seen in years. I realized that I could trust Karen with my most painful thoughts and emotions, and that she would never use those things against me. And the deeper I let her in, the closer we became.

Eventually we learned to share our struggles with other couples from church, and each time we did it got a little easier. And people never judged or mocked us. Most would respond by telling some of the struggles they had been dealing with in their marriage. We learned the value of support systems and how important it is for people to pray for each other and hold each other accountable.

We learned the freedom and healing that comes from letting others in. We learned the power of vulnerability and humility. We learned the strength that can only be found through meekness.

Confess to One Another

If you've never allowed yourself to experience the freedom that comes from lifting the veil and letting others inside the deepest, most painful parts of yourself, I challenge you to do so today.

Begin by learning to open up to your spouse. Remove your self-imposed mask and allow them to see the part of you that you've worked so hard to keep hidden. Trust them with your pain, with your insecurities, with your struggles. Trust them with the secrets of your past. Trust them with the wounds that remain hidden deep in the hurt pocket of your spirit. Give them the chance to be the loving and caring partner that you most need in a spouse. Open your heart and let them in.

And if you struggle with a crippling and hidden sin or addiction, find a trusted friend or pastor in whom you can confide. Find someone who will be there for you, who will walk with you through your struggles, who is solid enough to hold you accountable. Find someone who will support you in prayer and keep your confessions in strict confidence. Someone who will be there when you most need them. Confess your sins so that God can begin the healing process.

Don't live another minute in fear and doubt. Trust God with your heart and come out of hiding.

Begin today by cooperating with God, and let him begin a miracle in your heart and life. He can heal your pain and set you free, but only if you open up and let him in.

 Takeaway

- God can heal any wound, no matter how deep or painful. But he first needs us to come out of hiding and begin owning those struggles that hold us hostage to sin or insecurity or dysfunction.

- Karen and I had a lot of struggles in the early years of our marriage, and most of them were caused by our inability to process and confess our pain and insecurities to each other.

But it is through brokenness that God brings healing. It is only when we learn to open up to each other that God is able to step in and redirect the course of our lives.

- James 5:16 says, "Therefore confess your sins to each other and pray for each other so that you may be healed." Scripture teaches that there is supernatural healing to be found through humility and vulnerability.

—10—

Do You Want to Be Well?

God never allows pain without a purpose in the lives of His children.

—*Jerry Bridges*

Although it is sometimes difficult for us to believe, God uses all of the events of our lives to prepare us for the future.

—*Charlyn Singleton*

Years ago, we had a customer who came in regularly to my dad's appliance store while I was still working there. She must have had a serious memory problem, because she could never remember anyone's name.

Every time she walked up to the counter I would greet her with a smile, and she would look at me and say, "Who are you?" I could never get used to that, because I had known her for years. I had even been at her house several times to deliver and install appliances. But she never seemed to remember me.

In fact, she could never seem to remember anything. She'd forget why she came in, what she was looking for, and even where she was. A sale that would normally take ten or fifteen minutes would often take several hours with this woman. No one wanted to wait on her, because it could get pretty frustrating. But my dad was always extremely patient with her. I'm guessing that's why she kept coming in.

Years later, while serving as the senior pastor of Trinity Fellowship Church in Amarillo, I looked across the crowd one day and saw this same woman sitting in the audience. I'd had no idea she attended our church, but I was glad to see her.

I soon learned that one of the other pastors had been working with her for several years. Once a week she would come to the building to meet with him, and he would help balance her checkbook and make sure she was paying her bills on time, keeping up with her appointments, and taking her medication. Basically, he just helped her navigate the daily tasks and details of life.

When this pastor was scheduled to leave for a six-month mission trip, he asked if I'd be willing to take care of the woman while he was gone. He knew I had known her for years and thought she might feel comfortable dealing with me. I was somewhat reluctant, but I agreed to help him out.

During our first meeting, it felt like old times. She walked into my office and sat down. I smiled and told her hello, then she looked at me and said, "Who are you?"

I spent the first few minutes reminding her that we had known each other for years and that I was going to be helping her out for the next few months. Then we got down to business. She explained everything she could remember about her finances, appointments, and other details I needed to know.

A few minutes later I was looking over her checkbook, and she again looked at me and asked, "Who are you?"

Now, I know I'm supposed to be patient and pastoral in these circumstances, but something in the way she looked at me made me wonder if there wasn't more going on upstairs than she was willing to let on. So I laid her checkbook on the table and said to her, "You know what's amazing to me? You remembered everything about this meeting. You remembered where the church was, you remembered where to park, you remembered how to find my office, you even remembered what time we were supposed to meet. So I don't think your memory is really that bad."

I paused for a minute to see if she would respond, but she didn't say a word. So I continued.

"So here's what we're going to do for the next six months. I'm going to help you, but I want you to drop the act. I want you to deal honestly with me, and I promise I'll be honest with you. And I'll help you all I can for the next six months."

She slowly nodded, and we went on with our meeting.

For the next six months, she never once asked me who I was or what she was doing there. She remembered every meeting and never gave me an ounce of trouble. In fact, I was surprised to find how intelligent and witty she was. She might have been smarter than me. She and I became good friends during that time.

Then one day the other pastor came back. He thanked me again for taking care of her while he was gone, then I filled him in on some of the details he needed to know about her finances and appointments.

The very next week, the woman came back to the building for her regular meeting and I saw her in the hallway. I smiled and said, "Hello, how are you today?"

She looked at me and asked, "Who are you?"

At that moment I realized something that had never quite dawned on me before. This poor woman had been emotionally sick for so long that her sickness had become far more than a mental dysfunction. It had become the defining characteristic of her life.

"Crazy" was not just her condition; it was her identity.

Defined by Pain

One of the biggest problems with being sick or dysfunctional or in pain is that it takes so much time and energy. Sickness has a way of consuming our thoughts and engulfing our spirits.

When someone is dealing with internal pain and distress, it tends to affect every area of their existence. Often it is all they think about. They lie awake at night worrying about their problem or sulking over the offense they suffered. And when they wake up, it's the first thing that comes into their mind. It takes tremendous energy to process the emotional roller coaster that pain brings into our lives.

The same is true with physical illness. When someone develops cancer, fighting the cancer quickly becomes his or her full-time job. When they're not physically dealing with their sickness, they're emotionally dealing with it, researching online, reading books about the latest cures, or just sitting in a chair worrying. Sickness can be devastating to both the body and the mind.

And sickness can easily become more than just a sickness; it can become our identity. It becomes who we are and how we see ourselves and our role in the world.

Jesus once ran across such a man at the Pool of Bethesda.

Bethesda was a place in Jerusalem with five porches and a large pool, and sick people would gather there daily, hoping to get healed. It was believed that an angel would come down into the pool at a certain time each day and stir the water, and when that happened, the first person into the pool would be healed of whatever disease or sickness they had.

This particular man had been at the pool every day for most of his life, but he had never been able to make it into the water for healing. He couldn't walk and was an invalid.

Jesus saw the man and learned that he had been coming there for a long time. As he approached the man, he asked, "Do you want to get well?" (John 5:6).

What an awkward thing to ask! Who does that? Who would ask a sick person such an obvious and insensitive question? If the man didn't want to be well, what would he be doing at the pool every day?

I can't imagine going to visit a sick friend at the hospital and saying to them as they lay there in bed, "Do you really want to get well?"

What sick person doesn't want to be free from their sickness? Who doesn't want to be well?

You and I both know that Jesus wasn't being insensitive. And he certainly wasn't mocking the poor man. Jesus simply had an intuitive understanding of human nature. He knew how easy it was for sickness to become more than a sickness. He understood that after thirty-eight years of being known as the invalid beside the pool, this man had almost certainly allowed his disability to become his identity.

Jesus was able and eager to heal the man. But first he wanted to hear from the man's own lips that he was ready and willing to be changed. That he was ready to start taking responsibility for his life and stop seeing himself as that sick guy by the pool.

There are three truths about divine healing that Scripture teaches, and all three of those truths are revealed in this simple story.

Healing Is a Partnership

The first truth is this: Healing is more than an act of God; it's a partnership that we enter into with God.

Before Jesus healed the man, he wanted him to understand the change that healing would bring about in his life. So he asked him, "Do you want to get well?"

Are you ready to put your sickness behind you? Are you ready for a new future? Are you ready to stop feeling sorry for yourself and get on with your life? Are you ready to pick up your mat, leave the pool, and begin seeing yourself as a healed person?

"Do you want to get well?"

God only works in our lives when he has our cooperation. Jesus never once healed a person against their will. He wanted them to participate in the process.

When Jesus was entering Jericho one day, a blind man threw off his cloak and ran to him for healing. But before Jesus healed the man, he asked him, "What do you want me to do for you?" (Mark 10:51).

He was willing to heal the man, but not before getting the man's participation.

John records another time when a blind man came to Jesus for healing, but instead of simply restoring the man's sight, Jesus made some mud with saliva and placed it on the man's eyes. Then he told him to go wash his eyes in the Pool of Siloam. The man did as Jesus asked and came home healed (see John 9:1–8).

Jesus could have healed the man by simply saying the words, but instead he wanted the man to partner with him in the healing. To be an active participant in the process.

Jesus didn't heal the man at the Pool of Bethesda until he was certain that the man was ready for healing. And afterward, Jesus said to him, "Get up! Pick up your mat and walk" (John 5:8).

Immediately the man realized he was healed, and he grabbed his mat and stood up.

The man was taking a risk by obeying Jesus. If you haven't stood in thirty-eight years, trusting your legs for the first time is a dangerous thing to do. At the very least it had to be a frightening thought. But Jesus didn't help the man up. He wanted him to stand up on his own.

He also expected him to pick up his own mat and leave.

Jesus was saying to the man, "This is no longer your spot. Once you get up you can't sit here anymore, so take your mat with you. It's time for you to start taking responsibility for your life."

One of the biggest problems with being sick is that it has a way of disabling our sense of responsibility. And that's true whether our sickness is internal or external. When we're dealing with pain, we can easily become dependent on others. And our dependency becomes more than a need; it becomes a lifestyle.

Jesus asked the man, "Do you want to get well?" because he knew that getting well would change everything for him. He would no longer be able to look to others for his basic needs. He'd probably have to go home and get a job, because no one wants to take care of a fully capable grown man. This was not an idle question on Jesus's part. He wanted the man to know the consequences of getting well. Jesus was asking, "Are you sure this is what you want?"

If you've found yourself bound by pain or depression or addiction, and you've been praying for God to heal you, maybe he's waiting until he knows you're fully committed to the partnership. Maybe he's waiting until you are truly ready to be healed. Maybe he's waiting for you to take the first step.

So often we want God to step in and heal our lives without taking any personal responsibility for our healing. We pray fervently for healing, but we never take time to ask God if there's something he needs us to do to partner with him in the process.

I know people who struggled for years with a drinking problem. They knew their problem was serious, and they were often brought to the point of brokenness and repentance on the heels of a drinking binge. But it was only when they finally came to the end of themselves and admitted that they needed help that God began the healing process. They took responsibility for their addiction and began attending AA meetings, and God came alongside and helped them get well.

Sometimes in order to be healed, we have to first mobilize ourselves to action.

A friend of mine once developed a chronic illness, and he dealt with it for years. He was a strong man of God and a mature Christian, and he approached his sickness with a great deal of faith. He asked for the prayers of our church, and people began meeting each week to pray for him. He wasn't getting any better, but through the entire ordeal his faith remained strong.

After several years his illness continued to progress, and soon he was no longer able to function normally. His body was shutting down, and he became disabled.

One day I was meeting with him and he confessed that he hadn't prayed about his sickness for some time. "The longer I was sick, the more it just kind of engulfed me," he said.

Then one morning he woke up and realized that his sickness had become his identity. He told me that he didn't pray for himself anymore. He just left that to his wife and those she had enlisted to pray. Instead of struggling to get well or trusting God to heal him, he had allowed his identity to be wrapped up in his disease. And that was the day he made the decision to come out of his apathy and "become militant." Those were his exact words. His spirit rose up inside of him and said, "I refuse to let this sickness overtake me! I refuse to give up. In the name of Jesus, I declare healing over my life!"

That began a major breakthrough in his healing process, and today he is completely healed of his illness.

Sometimes it takes a little righteous anger for healing to begin. Sometimes God is simply waiting for us to get serious enough to partner with him in our treatment. Healing is much more than an act of God. It's a process of teamwork and cooperation.

Healing Is a Lifestyle

The second truth about divine healing is that it is not an event; it's a lifestyle.

After Jesus healed the man by the Pool of Bethesda, he slipped away into the crowds. And later, when he saw the man in the temple, he approached him and said, "See, you are well again. Stop sinning or something worse may happen to you" (John 5:14).

We can't know for certain why the man was sick, but Jesus seems to be implying that it was sin that caused the man to become an invalid. I've known churches and pastors who teach that sickness is always caused by sin, and they use passages like this to prove their point. But I don't believe that's true. Most sicknesses are the result of unhealthy eating, too much stress, genetics, or living in a corrupted world.

But there are times when sickness is caused by sin. That was true in Jesus's day, and it's true today. And this man had apparently been sick because of his previous sins. So Jesus said to him, "Stop sinning or something worse may happen to you."

When Jesus decides to heal us, he expects a change in the way we've been living, because divine healing is not an event, it's a lifestyle. Jesus doesn't heal so that we can go back to our old habits. He heals in order to give us a victorious and righteous future.

A friend of mine has a national healing ministry, and I had lunch with him recently. He said to me, "Jimmy, whenever we have meetings, we see a tremendous number of people find miraculous healing."

It was encouraging to hear how God was blessing his ministry. But then he said, "Our biggest problem is, over half the people that we see getting healed are losing their healing, because they immediately go back to the same way they had been living."

We all tend to be creatures of habit. There's security in familiarity. Most of us enjoy regular routines. We like to frequent the same coffee shops, eat at the same restaurants, even sit in the same sections at church each week. There's comfort in doing things that feel familiar to us.

But when it comes to bad habits and negative patterns of behavior, we can't allow ourselves to get comfortable. Divine healing is available to us, but if we expect God's healing to remain, we have to be willing to change those lifestyle habits that caused us to be in bondage to pain.

When God stepped in and healed our marriage, Karen and I both felt him working supernaturally to heal our broken spirits. But we also knew that if our marriage was going to stay healed, we would both need to change the way we had been treating each other.

The dysfunction in our marriage was caused by our damaging and sinful behavior. I acted as an emotional bully, and that's why Karen was so wounded. God was willing to heal those wounds, but I had to completely change my way of relating to her for that healing to stay. Otherwise every area God had healed would have reverted to the way it had been.

Healing was a process. I had to learn new patterns of behavior, and so did Karen. We had to walk with God through the process, and we had to do our part. It wasn't an event; it was a change of lifestyle. By the time our marriage was completely healed, Karen and I were different people. We had developed new habits, new customs, new behavioral patterns, and an entirely different vocabulary toward each other.

So often people say to God, "Please heal our finances." But what they're really asking is, "God, please give us more money." God is willing to bless us financially, and he wants to do that, but the primary reason people don't have money is that they don't know how to manage the money they have.

If that has been your prayer, here's a news flash for you: God is not going to help you win the lottery. He's not going to plant an oil well in your front yard. He's not going to drop a bucket of money in your lap.

What he will do is come alongside you as you work with him to heal your financial problems.

struggle or affliction you are going through, remember that partnership. It isn't a onetime event. It's a change in lifestyle eeds us to embrace as we walk with him through the process.

Healing Is about Redeeming God's Purpose

The third truth about divine healing is perhaps the most critical of the three. God doesn't heal to simply relieve us of our pain; he heals in order to redeem his purpose for our lives.

The sick man by the Pool of Bethesda was not created to spend his days there beside the pool. He was created to glorify God. And nothing about his former life of sickness was glorifying. God is not glorified by seeing his people in bondage to sin and sickness and poverty.

God is glorified when we allow him to come in and redeem us from our sickness. God is glorified when you and I finally come out of our sin and shame and let him have his way in our lives. When we come out of hiding and say to God, "I can't do this on my own. Heal me, Lord! Heal my nakedness so I can live for you!"

God is glorified when we turn our brokenness into a testimony of his goodness and grace.

So often we feel overwhelmed by the brokenness that life has brought our way.

We think to ourselves:

God could never use someone like me.

I'm just a struggling alcoholic.

I've been divorced.

I've had an abortion.

I've been through bankruptcy.

I'm addicted to drugs.

I've got too many tattoos.

I'm just a sinner.

I could never reach anyone for Jesus.

I'm too broken to be any good to God.

But those are all lies from the enemy. In God's economy, our brokenness is his greatest asset. Through brokenness, God is able to redeem us. Then he uses our scars to reach others.

Your scars are your greatest testimony of God's ability to heal. And once you've been healed, once you've been redeemed from darkness, God uses your scars for his divine purposes.

No one understands sex addiction like someone who has been there. No one understands the pain and shame that may come with an unwanted pregnancy like someone who has experienced it or has been through an abortion. No one understands the hopelessness of depression like someone who has been rescued from the bottom of that pit. No one understands the trap of drug or alcohol addiction like someone who has been freed from it.

God heals in order to redeem his purpose for our lives.

Jesus didn't heal the man at the Pool of Bethesda to simply give him back his legs. He healed in order to give him a testimony and a renewed purpose for his life.

And he does the same for you and me.

A Redeemed Scar

Several weeks ago as I was greeting people between services, a woman I've known for years approached me. I knew she had recently lost her husband, so I told her I was sorry for her loss.

She said to me, "You know, the Lord told me years ago that I would someday have a ministry to widows. And I knew at the time that my husband would have to precede me in death for that to happen. I'm devastated by the loss of my husband, but I'm going to use my circumstances to help other widows."

I was amazed at her faith in the wake of devastation and heartache. An event that could have easily become a crippling depression instead became a powerful testimony of God's supernatural redemption.

Being a widow was her condition, but she didn't allow it to become her identity. She called on God to heal her pain and use her scars for his divine purposes. She allowed her healing to become her testimony.

Whatever pain or tragedy you are struggling to get through, whatever circumstance feels too overwhelming for you to endure, whatever sickness or addiction you've been fighting to overcome, trust the Hurt Redeemer to heal you.

Trust God to restore what the enemy has tried to destroy. He can heal your brokenness and use your scars to reach others.

Don't let your pain become your identity. Rather, let it be your testimony.

Takeaway

- Emotional pain and sickness have a way of consuming our thoughts and overwhelming our time and energy. When not dealt with, pain and dysfunction can become more than our condition; they can become our identity.

- Scripture teaches three truths about divine healing: (1) Healing is a partnership between us and God. (2) Healing is a lifestyle and demands a change in the way we live. (3) Healing is about redeeming God's purpose for our lives.

- God is glorified when we allow him to redeem our scars for his glory. He often uses our painful experiences as a testimony of his power to heal.

—11—

Lord of the Brokenhearted

How else but through a broken heart may Lord Christ enter in?

—*Oscar Wilde*

The LORD is close to the brokenhearted and saves those who are crushed in spirit.

—*Psalm 34:18*

James and Kyla seemed like the perfect couple.

James was a successful architect who ran his own company. He made a good living and was a doting father to his kids. Kyla was an ophthalmologist who had decided to put her career on hold to stay home with the children.

They lived in a nice house in the suburbs, had several good friends from church, and appeared to have a wonderful marriage.

But when they came to me for counseling, I was reminded again that looks can be deceiving. Kyla was on the verge of filing for divorce.

At Kyla's request, James wasn't present during our first counseling session. I spent the first twenty minutes getting to know her a little better and gaining a sense of their background as a couple. Then I asked her why she thought divorce was the only answer.

Kyla didn't really know how to respond. She gave a lot of vague answers, such as "I don't really love James anymore" and "I guess I'm just now willing to face the truth."

But she never really got to the heart of her frustration. So I posed a more specific question.

"Kyla, what caused you to fall out of love with James?"

With that, a well of emotion boiled to the surface. She started to answer but then suddenly lowered her head and broke down in a flood of tears. For several minutes she cried uncontrollably, with her head buried in her hands. Eventually her tears died down enough for her to speak.

"I can't take the pain any longer of being second to James's work," she said. "I complained for years and did everything I knew to do to attract James to me, but it didn't help. Every time I said something, he just tried to make me feel guilty about putting more pressure on him. Every time I complained and he rejected me, it just drove us farther apart. I don't believe he will ever change!"

Like a lot of wives, Kyla felt disconnected from her husband because of his busy schedule. It's a dynamic I've seen hundreds of times in my office. Husbands become so caught up in the stress of juggling the demands of their career with the needs of their family, that they soon lose perspective. It's a common trap that a lot of men fall into.

And my hunch was confirmed when I had a chance to meet with James. He admitted that he had been working long hours and that it was wrong for him to do so. And he acknowledged that he had been neglecting his marriage. But he was also dealing with a lot of his own frustrations in the relationship.

When Kyla quit her job it put a financial strain on their family, but James was committed to letting her stay home with the kids. Along with their mortgage and other monthly bills, he also had a large school loan to pay off. So James was forced to work longer hours in order to pay for it. He told me he was happy to do so, but from his perspective it was Kyla who worried most about their finances.

"Kyla would bring up the issue with my college loans in a way that always made me feel guilty," he said. "It made me angry and it became a sticking point in our relationship."

James confessed that he deeply resented Kyla for making him feel guilty about his student loans, and each time she brought the matter up it drove a deeper wedge between them. Then one day he came home from work to find that she had borrowed money from her parents to pay off the loan without asking him.

"I felt totally violated," James said. "That was several years ago, and she has never agreed that she was wrong."

In James's mind, Kyla's actions were a monumental breach of trust. And no matter how much he tried to explain his feelings to her, she never quite understood.

"Maybe that's why I find excuses to work so much," he said in frustration.

When Pain Finds You

Like so many of us, James and Kyla began their relationship with lofty dreams and high expectations. They were so in love when they met that they couldn't imagine anything ever coming between them. They were both young and attractive and educated, with the whole world at their feet. *A match made in heaven*, they thought.

But then the realities of life started to come at them from every side. Soon there were kids to feed, a mortgage to pay, a lawn to mow, a business to build. Before they knew it, they'd completely lost touch with each other. Their marriage became fractured and disenfranchised, their lives became chaotic and lonely, and their hearts became deeply and severely broken.

And the worst thing about being brokenhearted is you begin to feel like no one could possibly understand. You begin to think that no one can really relate to what you're going through. That you are completely helpless and alone, and that no one is really able to come alongside and meet the need.

James and Kyla aren't the only brokenhearted people in the world. We've all felt the sting of hopelessness and despair at some point in our lives.

Maybe you've felt it at the death of a loved one. You found yourself standing over a closed casket at a quiet graveside, wondering how and why God would allow someone to be taken before their time. *But they were so young. They had their whole life ahead of them. Why, God? Why?*

Maybe it came while sitting in the doctor's office. You had just gone in for a routine checkup, and now several visits later you find yourself sitting in a cold exam room waiting for results from the latest round of tests. Suddenly the doctor walks in and the news isn't good. *Why me, Lord? How am I going to tell my family?*

Maybe you sensed it at your accountant's office. You'd been struggling to keep your business afloat in a terrible economy, and you thought things were going better. The numbers were up, you'd just had a decent quarter, and you'd hoped your company had turned a corner. But the final numbers don't lie, and suddenly you're forced to face your greatest fear. "I think bankruptcy might be your only option," he tells you.

A dream dies and your heart breaks. And you have no idea how you'll ever go on.

Satan's Greatest Threat

Someone once said, "Show me a man's wounds and I'll show you his purpose."

Satan always attacks hardest at the point of our greatest gifting. And much of the pain we go through can be traced directly to the enemy's hatred for God. Satan hates God, and he hates any plans God has for our future.

That's why pain often hurts so deeply. The Hurt Whisperer is quick to capitalize on life's most catastrophic events.

Like a self-serving politician, Satan never lets a good tragedy go to waste.

Satan also feels most threatened where you and I are most gifted. Whenever he sees someone born with a unique talent or ability, he instinctively understands that God must have a special purpose in mind for that person. And that becomes the focus of his most prolific attacks.

Anytime you see a young man with a talent for music and songwriting, you can bet that his gift has been or will be attacked. You can be sure he has been mocked and ridiculed by others, maybe even heckled by friends, or chastised by those closest to him. In one form or another, his gift for music has brought him pain or insecurity or doubt.

Whenever you see a young girl with a special gift of compassion and kindness, you can be sure that she has been wounded deeply, often by those she is trying to help. In some strange way she has been made to feel small and insignificant because of her desire to reach out, and she has likely even been tempted to turn her back on those in need.

Wherever you see a special talent or desire, you can be sure that the devil has been hard at work. Because Satan never allows God's gifting to go unpunished.

And God often allows the pain in order to prepare us for his purpose.

God has a dream for your life, and he has a dream for mine. And realized dreams are almost always the product of gifts and wounds working together in the human heart. God uses both to make us into what he wants us to become.

Strength in Weakness

My life today is dedicated to strengthening marriages. Karen and I spend a lot of time ministering to couples in need of help or counseling. We have given our lives to the ministry of helping couples build strong and lifelong relationships with each other. It is more than a job or a ministry to us; it is our passion. It is what God called us to do. It is the greatest gift we could possibly give to the body of Christ.

I'm often called to speak on a number of topics, and I enjoy doing so, but marriage is the subject that most excites me. Because when I talk about bringing broken marriages back from the brink of divorce, the message is more than a well-researched outline on paper. It's a personal testimony.

I was called to preach at a young age, and I did that for many years, but I can now see that God's ultimate purpose for my life was to save struggling marriages. My greatest gifting is in helping hurting couples pick up the pieces of their shattered relationships and put them back together again.

And people tend to listen when I speak, because they know that I speak from experience. My words have credibility because I have been through many of the struggles they are facing.

During the early days of our marriage, Satan attacked us relentlessly. He used the pain of our past to try to tear our relationship apart. We felt his assaults on our marriage at every turn.

But God redeemed our marriage. God brought us back from the brink of disaster, and in the process he gave us a new dream. A new hope. A renewed sense of purpose for our lives and ministry. And today he uses our scars to help others. He uses our past to help hurting couples build a bright and purposeful future.

God is strongest where you and I are weakest. God is most able where you and I are most damaged. God is most glorified when you and I are the most broken and humble.

"For when I am weak, then I am strong," wrote the apostle Paul (2 Cor. 12:10).

God loves a broken pot, because it's through brokenness that we come face-to-face with our own humanity. Through brokenness we are forced to admit our complete inability to make it on our own. Through brokenness we finally see our need for Jesus.

Close to the Brokenhearted

With God, there is hope even in the midst of the worst possible news. Even in the midst of sickness or bankruptcy, there is reason to be optimistic. Even in the midst of death, there is resurrection.

The prophet Isaiah writes,

> The Spirit of the Sovereign LORD is on me, because the LORD has anointed me to proclaim good news to the poor. He has sent me to bind up the brokenhearted, to proclaim freedom for the captives and release from darkness for the prisoners, to proclaim the year of the LORD's favor . . . to comfort all who mourn, and provide for those who grieve in Zion—to bestow on them a crown of beauty instead of ashes, the oil of joy instead of mourning, and a garment of praise instead of a spirit of despair. (Isa. 61:1–3)

The true beauty of a relationship with God is that it can wipe away any amount of sorrow, overcome any failure, and erase any type of fear. God's good news trumps any bad news that could possibly come our way.

When your heart is broken and your dream destroyed, God is there to bring healing and restoration. He heals your heart and restores the dream you thought you had lost. In the midst of pain and sorrow, God promises beauty.

"The LORD is close to the brokenhearted and saves those who are crushed in spirit," writes the psalmist (Ps. 34:18). There is no pain too deep that God cannot heal it. No amount of sorrow that he cannot console. No amount of suffering that he cannot ease. No amount of brokenness that he cannot repair.

God's promises to us through the prophet Isaiah are not vague. And they are meant for every person who finds themselves in the midst of pain and sorrow and looks to God for help.

Good News to the Poor

"The LORD has anointed me to proclaim good news to the poor."

There is no pain that feels more hopeless than the pain of poverty. And that's true whether your poverty is financial or spiritual. Both leave you feeling completely helpless and alone.

If you don't know Jesus, you are living in a state of utter powerlessness and vulnerability before the enemy. Spiritual poverty is the worst type of poverty I can imagine. Living life without the guidance of the Holy Spirit and without the truth of God's Word in your heart is a devastating state to be in. Perhaps it feels so hopeless because it is.

You and I don't have the ability to overcome on our own. We don't have the tools to withstand the struggles of life, or the power to deal with pain and sorrow and chaos. Without God, we are destined to a life of failure and frustration. Without God, we can never find healing for the wounds that keep us in bondage to Satan.

But Jesus came to eliminate spiritual poverty. Jesus came to bring good news for those who don't know him! Jesus brings hope to anyone who will simply call on his name and trust him with the future. Jesus is close to the brokenhearted and saves those who are crushed in spirit. For those who are bound by spiritual poverty, there is hope and salvation found in the arms of Jesus. That is a promise from God that no amount of sin or waywardness can take away. Nothing can keep you from being forgiven and accepted by God.

And for those who are bound by financial poverty, God's promise of blessing is universal and nonnegotiable. God is a God of abundance and sufficiency. You were not meant to live in want or need. You were not meant to live in constant worry or frustration. You were not meant to live in lack. God has promised to provide, and when you give your cares to him, you will not be forsaken.

So many people live in fear and apprehension because they have not trusted God with their finances. They surrender their hearts to Jesus but try to remain in control of their money and possessions. But that doesn't work. God needs your complete trust, in every area of life. He needs your full surrender. He needs hands that are completely empty and submitted in order to bring the full extent of his blessing.

When you give God all that you are and all that you have, then all that he is and all that he has becomes yours.

"The LORD is my shepherd, I lack nothing," writes David. "You anoint my head with oil; my cup overflows" (Ps. 23:1, 5).

You were designed to live a life of abundance and grace. In God's hands you will never be in want.

Bind Up the Brokenhearted

For those who are brokenhearted, who have had a dream taken away, who have found themselves in the midst of confusion or doubt or devastation, God has promised to bind you up. To fix your heart. To give you back your dream. To calm your doubts. To restore what you've lost in the devastation of life.

"He has sent me to bind up the brokenhearted." Are there any among us who haven't experienced a broken heart?

There was a time when I was certain my marriage was over. Karen and I felt so disillusioned and disenfranchised that neither of us thought our marriage could possibly survive. We had wounded each other deeply and were certain that we had done irreparable harm to the relationship.

There were so many nights when we would go to bed angry, and I would lie awake wondering why we even kept trying. Our marriage felt so hopeless and lost, like an endless desert without a drop of water in sight. In our stubbornness and immaturity, we had brought such destruction to our relationship that I was convinced we had damaged it beyond repair.

And Karen felt the same way. She had felt so wounded and hurt by my domineering personality that she had emotionally shut down. She went into her own world and kept me at a safe distance. Each time we touched I could feel her flinch. My stubborn spirit and overpowering words had all but destroyed any love she ever felt for me.

There was a time when we both thought divorce was inevitable, and days when we both would have welcomed the idea with open arms. But God is a God of restoration. God is a God of hope and healing. God is a God who can bind up even the most broken and battered heart!

At the point of our greatest brokenness, Karen and I both raised the white flag of surrender. We gave our marriage to God, and he brought supernatural healing. He brought grace and forgiveness beyond anything we could have dreamed or imagined. He not only healed our fractured hearts; he gave us a sense of renewed love for each other that is greater than either of us could have ever envisioned.

There is good news for the brokenhearted! Good news for those who

> think their marriage can never be saved;
>
> believe they will never succeed;
>
> think their health will never get better;
>
> fear their businesses will fail or their careers will falter;
>
> think they will never find the right spouse;
>
> struggle with sickness or tragedy, with the loss of a friend, with the death of a child, with their parents' divorce, with spiritual and financial bankruptcy;
>
> think their life is over.

There is hope to be found in the chaos. There is restoration to be found in the midst of brokenness.

God is not finished with you yet. God has not given up or turned his face away. God has not forsaken you. Anything the devil has done, God can undo. Any pain the enemy has inflicted, God can heal. Any dream that Satan has crushed, God can restore.

Death could not keep Jesus in the grave, and it can't keep you there either!

For those who are brokenhearted, God is ready to bind you up and bring healing.

Freedom for the Captives

For those who have found themselves in bondage, struggling against the chains of addiction or depression or sin, God brings the hope of freedom.

"The Lord has anointed me . . . to proclaim freedom for the captives and release from darkness for the prisoners."

There is no prison that feels as dark and dreadful and hopeless as the prison of sin. There is nothing as helpless and frustrating as living in bondage to lust or anger or pornography, as being so entrapped by the devil's web of lies and deceit that you see no way of escape.

Sin is an unrelenting and merciless master. Once it has you in its claws, it clamps down hard and doesn't let go. And it leaves no part of you unscathed or unaffected. It seeps into your heart and spirit and begins corrupting your soul from the inside out.

I've seen grown men brought to their knees in tears of regret over the sin of lust. They began dabbling in pornography, thinking it was a harmless little habit that wouldn't hurt anyone, convinced that no one would ever know. But their occasional sin soon became a full-fledged addiction. It became a beast that wouldn't let go of their hearts and minds. And now they find themselves completely helpless to overcome their addiction on their own.

Others have found themselves bound by drugs or alcohol or depression, or perhaps a serious eating disorder. Some are bound by the chains of sexual addiction or promiscuity or adultery.

Maybe your chains are more socially acceptable, like the chains of greed or envy or materialism. Maybe you're bound by conceit or arrogance. Perhaps you struggle with gossip or judgmentalism or spiritual pride. Or maybe you have a propensity to justify your own sins while quickly condemning others.

Socially acceptable sins are arguably the worst kind, because they so often stay under the radar of conviction. We seldom see the harm they do—both to us and to those around us—so we let them slide and instead focus on the sins of others.

But in God there is freedom from the chains of captivity. In God, there is freedom from addiction, freedom from sin, freedom from anxiety and depression, freedom from any chain the enemy has used to keep your heart held hostage.

"Where the Spirit of the Lord is, there is freedom," writes the apostle Paul (2 Cor. 3:17).

Only God can remove the chains that bind you. Only God can truly set you free.

When Tragedy Strikes

When I first met James and Kyla they appeared to be the perfect couple. But I soon learned otherwise. They were just two broken pots trying desperately to make sense of their brokenness.

When they first met me they thought I was the perfect husband. They soon learned otherwise. I'm just a broken pot who has found supernatural healing at the hands of the Master Potter.

James and Kyla are still married, navigating their life as a couple. And every day they stay together they find more grace and restoration in the arms of Jesus. Their marriage grows stronger with each passing week. Maybe someday God will use their wounds to help others, just as he continues to use ours.

Perhaps God will use your scars as well. It all depends on what you allow him to do with your brokenness.

Takeaway

- We've all experienced the pain of being brokenhearted. Marriages struggle, loved ones pass away, people get sick, businesses go under, jobs are lost, and dreams die. No one gets through life unaffected by pain and heartache.

- Satan is quick to capitalize on catastrophic events when they come into our lives, and he uses them to try to tear us away from God.

- God also uses times of pain and heartache to "bind us up" and bring perspective to our lives.

- God brings good news to the brokenhearted and restoration in the midst of brokenness. Paul tells us, "Where the Spirit of the Lord is, there is freedom" (2 Cor. 3:17). Only God can remove the chains of bondage that hold us hostage to sin and dysfunction.

—12—

Beauty for Ashes

He has sent me . . . to bestow on them a crown of beauty instead of ashes.

—*Isaiah 61:1, 3*

Behold, I am making all things new.

—*Revelation 21:5 NASB*

Life doesn't always unfold the way we've planned. Sometimes tragedy finds us, often when we least expect it.

This past summer, many of my friends experienced that reality firsthand.

With the country facing the worst drought in over a decade, many western states were ravaged by wildfires. And some of the worst of those fires happened in Colorado.

When Karen and I heard the news that a fire raged out of control just west of Colorado Springs, the concern turned personal for our family. Our daughter, Julie, lives in Colorado Springs with her husband, Cory, and our precious twin granddaughters, Elle and Abby. We also have a lot of good friends and colleagues who live in the area, which only intensified our concern.

For several days the fires burned just west of the city, and with the winds blowing mostly to the north, it looked like Colorado Springs would be safe. Until one day, on a Tuesday afternoon, an unexpected windstorm from the west began pushing the fire toward the western edge of the city. The winds were slow at first but quickly began to pick up speed. Soon they were blowing at gusts of over sixty miles an hour.

Within minutes the firefighters had lost control of the blaze and were forced to pull back. Almost without warning, the fires crested the top of the Front Range and began racing toward town. The authorities issued an evacuation notice for the entire west side of the city, and the streets were suddenly logjammed with cars as people scrambled to leave their homes and reach safety. Before long, entire neighborhoods were engulfed in flames as the fire continued to rage out of control.

By that evening, more than thirty thousand residents had been displaced from their homes. Most stayed with friends and family, or in one of the few hotel rooms they could find, but many fled the city altogether.

My daughter and her family lived a safe distance away, so thankfully their home was not in the path of the fire, but the smoke was so thick and toxic that they decided to flee the city for the sake of their children's health. They drove to New Mexico to stay at their grandparents' home until it was safe to return.

Thousands of firefighters, many from neighboring cities and states, fought the blaze through the night and into the next morning, doing all they could to contain the fires and save as many homes as possible. When it was over, nearly 350 homes had been completely destroyed, and thousands more sustained some level of damage. Two elderly people were not able to evacuate in time, so they lost their lives in the fire. It was one of the worst disasters in Colorado history.

Friends who live in Colorado Springs describe the event as the most horrific scene they've ever witnessed. Many who were fleeing their homes made their way north on I-25 to escape the area, and as they looked back on the city the entire Front Range looked like a war zone. The western mountains were completely engulfed in flames. Smoke and ash rose up as far as the eye could see, consuming the landscape for miles in every direction. One friend said it was like Armageddon.

The days that followed are still a blur in the minds of many residents. Even those who were not affected by the fires were devastated by what they had witnessed. Almost everyone had a friend or family member who had lost their home or whose home had suffered some sort of damage. Many local businesses closed up shop for a few days, just to give their employees time to regroup after the devastation.

One friend described the atmosphere in town as something out of a bad horror film. People were wandering through the aisles of grocery stores in a zombielike state, almost as if they were in a trance. It was as if half the city was suffering from post-traumatic stress disorder. Time seemed to stand still as residents did their best to process what they had just experienced.

Where Was God?

Colorado Springs had become a city of the brokenhearted. And the entire town struggled to make sense of the seemingly senseless tragedy. Just about everyone seemed to be either in shock or angry. Many were left completely bewildered by the chaos and destruction, and some openly wondered why God would allow such a horrible thing to happen.

Why would God allow such a freak and unexpected windstorm just when the firefighters seemed to be getting the upper hand? Why did he not bring a torrent of rain to subdue the fires before they had time to do so much damage? Why did he not stop the fires before they reached the city, before they had a chance to destroy so many homes, before they had a chance to take the lives of two innocent people?

The sentiment is a common one, and the questions are not surprising. We've all heard them before. Anytime a tragedy or disaster strikes, people are left reeling in the chaos, asking themselves, "Where was God when this was happening? Why didn't he do something about it?"

When the terrorist attacks of 9-11 brought down the World Trade Center in New York, voices all over the globe rose up in anger and frustration, asking, "Why did God let this happen?"

Each time a crazed individual straps on an arsenal of guns and ammunition and sets out to open fire in a school or movie theater or military base, the senselessness of it all causes people to shake their fists at the sky and ask God, "Where were you when we needed you? Why didn't you stop this from happening?"

It's a question that God has heard countless times since the beginning of creation, each time tragedy or devastation comes into the world.

A father loses his son in a car accident at the hands of a drunk driver, and he lies awake at night, his pillow drenched in tears, his heart in agony from the pain. And he cries out to God, "Why, Lord? Why?"

A child sits alone on a bench outside the courtroom, waiting for her parents to finish their meeting with the lawyers, waiting to find out which one she'll be living with after the divorce. And her spirit cries out through the pain, "Why don't you care about me, God? Why are you letting this happen to me?"

The seemingly senseless tragedies of life have left us all a bit confused and baffled at some point in our lives. And in the darkness of desperation, we've all wondered in our hearts how a good and loving God could allow such pain.

Struggling with God

Few pastors want to tackle this topic head-on. When faced with questions about God's goodness, many choose to sidestep the issue with one of the canned responses we Christians often use: "It will all make sense in eternity." Or perhaps, "What Satan planned for harm, God will use for his purposes." And those are true statements.

But they still aren't really answers, are they?

Let's be completely honest with each other. We both know that God doesn't cause tragedy, but he does *allow* it to happen. He could stop it if he wanted to.

God could have stopped the fires. He could have said to the flames, "You can go this far, but no farther." He could have prevented every bit of the devastation.

God could have stopped the planes from hitting the towers of the World Trade Center. He could have stopped the terrorists before they ever had a chance to board the planes.

And God could stop every crazed gunman who ever set out to do harm. He could keep the tragedies from happening before any of them had the chance to happen.

If God couldn't do all of that and more, then he wouldn't be an all-powerful God. And you and I know that he is.

So why doesn't he?

As hard and harsh as it sounds, maybe God allows tragedy to come into our lives because tragedy is often the only thing that engages us with God. Maybe God allows heartbreak and chaos and confusion because through those things we finally begin to wake from our apathy and participate in humanity's most critical fight. We begin to struggle with God. We're shaken out of our indifference and roused to engage in the relationship, many of us for the very first time.

"Struggle with God is the essence of relationship with God," writes James Emery White, and many of us know exactly what he means. It is often through times of confusion or doubt or anger that we find ourselves looking to God for answers. We struggle to make sense of the world, and that struggle leads us to the foot of God's throne. And it is in the midst of that struggle that we often find him.

I once heard someone say that a believer's relationship with God is like a pendulum. And the pendulum is constantly swinging, first away from God and then toward him. Through the ups and downs of life we find ourselves first drifting away from God, then moving back toward his direction. At any given time we all find ourselves somewhere along the path of this spiritual and emotional pendulum.

I'm not sure I agree, but I understand the sentiment.

I think a better analogy might be a tug-of-war. Many of us find ourselves in a perpetual battle of wills with God, he on one end of the rope and we on the other, each struggling against the pull. As we pull away from God, struggling to get our way, he is constantly pulling us toward him. God is always fully engaged in the relationship, always pulling, always wooing, always drawing us closer. And the harder we pull, the closer he is able to draw us into the relationship.

It's only when we give up the struggle that we find ourselves in a state of indifference. When we stop fighting, stop tugging the rope, stop engaging with God, our relationship becomes stale and lazy and stagnant.

The same is true when it comes to sin. The sin nature inside of us doesn't like struggling with God, and when left to our own devices many of us would simply stop struggling and give in to temptation when it comes our way. The human side of us will always want to take the path of least resistance.

But God calls us to a higher standard. God expects us to fight our sin nature and engage with him in the struggle. To fight temptation when it comes. It is in the midst of that struggle that he is able to draw us away from our fallen nature and deeper into the relationship he longs to have with us.

It is through struggle that we find true intimacy with God.

The Scars of Our Struggles

Many of the struggles I've experienced in life have been physical. And I have the scars to prove it.

On my chin is a scar that I got at the age of five. One of my brothers (Damien, I think) pushed me off of our neighbor's flatbed truck and I hit a brick. I got a gash on my chin that bled for hours.

On the back of my right calf is another scar. A neighborhood friend once fashioned a spear out of a bamboo shoot and accidentally impaled me in the leg. It hurt so bad I almost cried. Almost.

I have a long, ugly scar on my right elbow. This one came from a surgery I had in the eighth grade. I had experienced a series of injuries to my elbow and a mass of damaged cartilage had developed, so the doctor had to go in and repair it.

Each time I see these scars I remember the physical pain I suffered when the injuries occurred. If it weren't for the scars, I probably would have forgotten the experiences altogether by now.

But I also have emotional scars on my spirit, and they are just as fresh in my memory. They are scars from the many spiritual and internal struggles I've been through.

I remember the pain I felt each time I was wounded and taken for granted as a child. Each time I suffered an injustice at the hands of a nameless, faceless school bureaucrat. Each time I was made fun of for my size, or that awful, enormous silver tooth the dentist put right in the front of my mouth. Each time someone called me "Bucky the Silver-toothed Beaver."

I remember each time I got swats in school for my rebellious attitude. The paddle may have landed on my backside, but the scars were left lingering in my heart and spirit.

I remember the pain I inflicted on Karen as a young married man. I remember the endless arguments we had in our struggle to navigate our new life together as a couple. I remember the times I took her for granted, the times I tried to control her, the times I wounded her tender self-image with my angry words, the times I tried to dominate the relationship because of my insecurity. The scars of regret are plentiful, and they remain fresh in the forefront of my mind.

God saved our marriage and renewed our love for each other. He brought healing and restoration to our hearts. He delivered me from the anger and resentment and insecurity that plagued me as a child, and he taught me how to be a better husband and father. He gave our family renewed hope and a glorious future.

But he left the scars to remind us of what we had been through. He left the scars so that we would never forget the pain and misery of our former lives. So that we would never forget the spiritual and emotional struggles that made us into the people he longed for us to become.

The Purpose of Our Scars

The prophet Isaiah wrote, "The LORD has anointed me . . . to comfort all who mourn, and provide for those who grieve in Zion—to bestow on them a crown of beauty instead of ashes, the oil of joy instead of mourning, and a garment of praise instead of a spirit of despair" (Isa. 61:1–3).

But what exactly does that mean?

It means God not only comforts us when we mourn and provides for us when we grieve; he actually takes our pain and turns it into pleasure. Out of the ashes of our lives he brings beauty. He takes our mourning and turns it into joy. And he takes our sorrow and despair and turns them into thoughts of praise.

He takes our struggles and turns them into an eternal and intimate relationship.

God uses the wounds and scars of life for his divine purposes. While he could deliver us from our pain, he often chooses to deliver us *through* it instead.

When Jesus appeared to his disciples after his resurrection, they recognized him from the scars on his hands, feet, and side. Jesus had just conquered death for all eternity. He had just gone to war with all the forces of hell and come out victorious. He had just sealed his enemy's eternal fate and had opened the door to eternal life for all who would put their trust in him.

It was history's most brutal and bloody battle, and Jesus won! But he didn't get through it without pain. The war brought suffering and sacrifice and agony. There were real tears on the cross. The pain and anguish were excruciating. The price being paid brought unimaginable torment to the body and spirit of Christ.

And when it was over, the battle was won but the scars remained. The scars that Jesus bore became divine markers of the war he had fought for souls, reminders of the pain and sacrifice, physical evidence of an epic and everlasting spiritual victory.

God leaves scars because scars are our constant reminders of what he was able to accomplish through us and within us. Scars become our testimony. Our wounds become souvenirs of the painful but freeing journey we took with God by our side.

Like little stone markers of our faith, these scars remain constantly before us, so that we will always remember the pain we've been through and the devastation from which God delivered us.

Stories of Hope

It has been quite awhile now since the fires raged in the city of Colorado Springs, and most residents have been able to go on with their lives. Most families have rebuilt and put their lives back together after losing everything they owned. Much of the confusion and anger has subsided, and instead people are focused on restoring the city back to normal.

But the stories following the fire are still fresh and alive. Many are just now unfolding.

After the fires, the city came together to help those who had lost their homes, and area churches were on the front lines of that battle. Hundreds of volunteers from those churches began showing up to help families sift through the rubble and ashes, searching for any trinkets or valuables that might still be found in one piece. The process was long and grueling, but volunteers continued to show up. It was really more about showing moral support than a search for usable items.

Most of the things they found were not that valuable. There were numerous clay cups and saucers, most of which were chipped and scarred, but had sentimental value nonetheless. Sometimes boxes of books or albums would be found beneath the ashes, often surprisingly intact. Beyond that there wasn't much they found that could be salvaged.

But amazingly, there was still beauty to be found amidst all the ashes. With each passing week, pastors all over the city were hearing stories of healing and restoration in the aftermath of the fire. There were stories of families who had been distant and disenfranchised from each other but had somehow found reconciliation in the wake of tragedy. Stories of teenage sons who had been caught up in drugs and alcohol but were brought to the point of repentance amidst the devastation. Stories of wayward children, detached fathers, apathetic mothers, fractured friendships, and alienated families who had found healing or restoration or perspective while sifting through the rubble of their lives.

Even in the midst of tragedy, God brings hope. Even in the midst of life's darkest hours, life's most chaotic seasons, our most baffling and confusing moments. Even in the midst of doubt and uncertainty, God brings renewal. Even in the midst of rebellion, God brings repentance.

"He has sent me to bind up the brokenhearted, to proclaim freedom for the captives and release from darkness for the prisoners."

Beauty for Ashes

Of all the stories that have unfolded since that fateful day in Colorado, there is one that most deeply moves me.

On the west side of Colorado Springs lived a profoundly wounded family. The parents had struggled for years to make their marriage work, but nothing seemed to help. At one point they tried counseling, but funds didn't allow them to keep going. So they continued to drift apart.

Two months before the fire, the couple decided to separate. He moved into an apartment across town. She took off her wedding ring and put it on the nightstand beside the master bed. The fate of their children and possessions were put in the hands of the divorce lawyers.

When the fires raged in the city, everything they had was lost. The home was completely incinerated.

A few weeks later, the family found themselves working alongside volunteers, sifting through the ashes of their possessions, searching for anything they could find that might have value. The husband worked on one side of the house while the wife worked on the other. Few words were exchanged between them.

While sifting through the basement ash, a volunteer stumbled upon a small shiny object. She picked it up and wiped off the soot. It was a wedding ring. Unaware of the family's struggles, she excitedly ran to the husband to show him what she'd found. Without saying a word he slipped it into his pocket and continued his search.

Late that afternoon, while volunteers were packing their things to leave, the husband saw his wife standing alone, so he approached her. Quietly, with tears forming in his eyes, he handed her the ring and asked a simple question.

"Could we please try again?"

And she said yes.

"He has sent me . . . to bestow on them a crown of beauty instead of ashes, the oil of joy instead of mourning, and a garment of praise instead of a spirit of despair."

Even in the midst of brokenness, God brings healing.

Takeaway

- When tragedy strikes, many of us find ourselves blaming God and wondering why he allowed it to happen when we know he could have prevented it.

- We all know that God can deliver us from our pain, but instead he often chooses to deliver us through it. God allows pain and turmoil because it is often during times of suffering that we're most engaged in the relationship. He uses tragedy to draw us to himself.

- The scars left behind on the heels of tragedy often become like stone markers, reminding us of God's power and provision in the midst of pain. God brings beauty from the ashes of our lives.

PART 4

Breaking the

Hurt Legacy

For I have chosen him, so that he will direct his children and his household after him to keep the way of the Lord by doing what is right and just.

—*Genesis 18:19*

One of the primary goals in our lives should be to prepare for our last day. The legacy we leave is not just in our possessions, but in the quality of our lives.

—*Billy Graham*

—13—

A Legacy of Pain

At the end of your life on earth you will be evaluated and rewarded according to how well you handled what God entrusted to you.

—*Rick Warren*

Dan is a tremendously gifted speaker and theologian. He knows the Bible better than most pastors and can speak on just about any topic he's asked to present. He's studied the Bible so much that he often doesn't even have to prepare.

He is so gifted in the pulpit that he can mesmerize just about any audience, one minute having them laughing uncontrollably at his jokes, and the next bringing the entire room to tears. I'd venture to guess that he's as good as any speaker you've ever heard. Maybe even better.

But even if I told you his real name, chances are slim that you've ever heard of him. For all his giftedness, Dan has made very little impact on the world for the kingdom of Christ. Those who are familiar with him likely know him best for the pain he's inflicted on his family and those around him. Dan is a deeply wounded person, and he's never really let God deal with his wounds. So as hard as he tries to make a name for himself, he leaves nothing but scorched earth in his path.

Throughout his ministry, Dan has had numerous adulterous affairs. And he always seems to get caught. Each time he is found out he confesses and is brought to his knees in repentance. He promises he'll never do it again, and people forgive him. But it's happened so many times that no one really believes Dan will change. He's left several churches in shame, but he quickly finds another place to minister. After all, Dan is a very gifted speaker.

Dan has also proven that he can't be trusted in business. Through the years he's made several jaunts into entrepreneurial ventures, and because of his quick wit and likable personality, he always seems to gain the confidence of others. But every one of his ventures has failed, and others are almost always left holding the bills. Dan has lost a lot of money through the years, and none of it ever seems to be his own.

A year ago, Dan's wife of nearly thirty years left him. She could no longer take the stress of constantly making excuses for her husband. And his children are all deeply wounded by their father's deceitful reputation.

A Painful Legacy

Dan grew up in a legacy of pain. And he has left a legacy of pain behind him.

This isn't what he was created to do, but it's what the enemy has accomplished through him. Dan has been brought to the point of brokenness many times, and no one doubts that his remorse is real. But for some reason he has never taken the necessary steps to let God truly heal the pain in his heart.

Each time Dan gets caught hurting others, he confesses and promises to change. But then as soon as the coast is clear, he goes back into hiding. He stuffs his pain back down, deep inside the hurt pocket of his spirit. He pretends that everything is fine and tries to go on with his life. But it's only a matter of time before the hurt and insecurity resurface. It's only a matter of time before Dan is once again wounding those around him.

We are all living between generations, and we all have two legacies that face us. The first is the legacy that has gone before us. And the second is the legacy we leave behind.

The legacy that has gone before us has a profound impact on who we are and what we have become. We are all, in some way, a product of our past.

And the legacy we leave will be profoundly impacted by who we are and what we choose to do. The generations to come will all, in some way, be a product of the past we leave behind.

The Bible teaches that we will all someday stand before God and give an account for our lives. Salvation comes only through our faith in Jesus, and that is never in question. But the rewards we gain in eternity will be based on what we've done with the time and grace God has given us. And those rewards will be decided at the judgment seat.

I'm convinced that when that day comes, we will not only give an account for our lives; we'll be held accountable for our legacy as well. It isn't just what we did with our lives that will matter; it is how our actions impacted our children, our grandchildren, and every future generation to come.

We will be judged by our legacy.

Jonathan and Max

In 1906 a study was released that compared the legacies of two very different men.

The first was a man named Jonathan Edwards. He was an evangelist in the eighteenth century who profoundly impacted the world for Christ. He is known today as the "Father of the Great Awakening," a revival that forever changed the course of religious history.

The second was a man named Max Jukes. Max also lived in the eighteenth century, but history knows him only as New York City's most shameless drunk.

By the year 1906, enough evidence had been compiled on both men to compare over a hundred years of their respective family legacies. And the findings were fascinating.

Jonathan Edwards and his wife, Sarah, had eleven children—three sons and eight daughters. Edwards was known as a man of tremendous humility and spiritual conviction. What he lacked in speaking ability, he more than made up for in his commitment to unashamedly preach the truth of God's Word. And Sarah is remembered as a woman of great faith and extraordinary beauty, who prayed incessantly for her children.

It was Edwards's famous sermon, "Sinners in the Hands of an Angry God," that is credited for sparking America's most powerful revival, known today as the Great Awakening.

But it is his legacy that many find most astonishing. Among Edwards's descendants were fourteen college presidents; more than a hundred college professors; more than a hundred lawyers; thirty judges; sixty physicians; more than a hundred clergymen, missionaries, and theology professors; sixty authors; three senators; and a vice president of the United States. Even those who conducted the study were dumbfounded by the extent of Edwards's amazing legacy.

Max Jukes's legacy was an entirely different story. Jukes never amounted to anything and left only pain in his wake. He also had many children, but they barely knew him. He would go off for days at a time on drunken binges, then return home in order to sober up. He spent most of his time asleep on the family couch.

By 1906, he had left behind three hundred descendants. And of those descendants, ten were living in poverty, a hundred and fifty were known criminals, a hundred were drunks, seven were murderers, and half of his female descendants were prostitutes. It was estimated that his descendants had cost the state of New York over twelve million dollars during the hundred years following Jukes's death. In today's economy, the cost would be an even more staggering amount of money.

Two different men. Two entirely different legacies.

Which would you rather leave behind?

The Story of Two Kings

In the Old Testament we read about two kings with very different stories. Both reigned over Israel and both were from the same bloodline, but the legacies they left behind couldn't have been more different.

The first is King Hezekiah. Hezekiah was a good king. He had a close relationship with God and made many religious reforms that pleased the Lord. For example, when he came to power he cleansed Judah of any visual reminders of their idol worship and lack of faith in God. He destroyed the altars, idols, and pagan temples they had built and reopened the Jewish temple in Jerusalem that his father had boarded up. Hezekiah was a righteous king; however, his faith was shortsighted. While he was concerned about the present state of things, for some reason he didn't have the wisdom or foresight to protect Judah's future.

Hezekiah was so proud of what he had accomplished in his kingdom that he put the wealth of Judah on display for the Babylonians, leading them to return years later to pillage the treasures God had given his people.

When the prophet Isaiah learned of Hezekiah's foolishness, he came to him with a warning from God.

> Hear the word of the LORD: The time will surely come when everything in your palace, and all that your predecessors have stored up until this day, will be carried off to Babylon. Nothing will be left, says the LORD. And some of your descendants, your own flesh and blood who will be born to you, will be taken away, and they will become eunuchs in the palace of the king of Babylon. (2 Kings 20:16–18)

When Hezekiah was informed of the tremendous suffering and hardship that would be brought on his descendants because of his sin, his reaction was almost unimaginable. Just look at his response:

> "The word of the LORD you have spoken is good," Hezekiah replied. For he thought, "Will there not be peace and security in my lifetime?" (v. 19)

Hezekiah actually rejoiced because he himself wouldn't have to suffer for the sins he committed. The curses he brought on his descendants wouldn't happen until after he was gone, and that was his most pressing concern.

King Hezekiah did a lot of good things in his life, but when it came to his legacy, he was surprisingly shortsighted. He was so focused on the present that he couldn't see past his own lifetime. And his lack of foresight brought pain and suffering to his descendants for generations after him.

Hezekiah's son was a young man named Manasseh. Considered to be the most evil king in the history of Judah, Manasseh turned the hearts of God's people toward sorcery, witchcraft, and divination, and he began erecting altars to Baal. He even sacrificed his own sons to fire in order to appease his false gods.

Scripture records that Manasseh "shed so much innocent blood that he filled Jerusalem from end to end" (2 Kings 21:16).

During King Manasseh's reign, he led Judah away from God and ushered in some of the darkest days in Jewish history. He undid all the good that his father had done for the nation. And when he died, he left his throne to his son Amon, who was just as evil and corrupt. Amon was assassinated only two years into his reign.

For nearly three generations Judah suffered the consequences of King Hezekiah's shortsightedness. Countless people paid the price for his sin of pride.

But God had mercy on Judah and decided to relieve them of their pain. And he did it by ushering in the reign of King Josiah.

Josiah was the son of Amon, and he was only eight years old when he became king of Judah. But his wisdom and righteousness far surpassed his age.

Josiah saw the wickedness of his fathers before him and wanted nothing to do with it. So he set out to tear down the pagan idols his predecessors had built. He removed all the shrines that had aroused the Lord's anger, and he rid Judah of the mediums and spiritists, the household gods, and all the other things that were detestable in the eyes of God.

Then he reinstated the Passover celebrations and restored Judah once again as a nation of God's chosen people.

Scripture records, "Neither before nor after Josiah was there a king like him who turned to the LORD as he did—with all his heart and with all his soul and with all his strength, in accordance with all the Law of Moses" (2 Kings 23:25).

Two very different kings. Two very different stories. Two very different legacies.

Sins of the Parents

God said to the people of Israel:

> I, the LORD your God, am a jealous God, punishing the children for the sin of the parents to the third and fourth generation of those who hate me, but showing love to a thousand generations of those who love me and keep my commandments. (Deut. 5:9–10)

The word that we translate as "sin" in this passage is the Hebrew word *avon*, and it means "to bend or twist." It can also be translated as "iniquity."

I grew up in the Texas panhandle, and we get a lot of wind blowing across the plains. As a result, many trees grow bent and twisted because of the constant pressure from the winds. Their environment makes it difficult for them to grow up straight.

I think that's a good analogy of what God was saying about the sin of the parents. When parents live in sin, it's like a constant wind pummeling the family, putting downward pressure on the children, making it nearly impossible for kids to grow up the way they should. So they grow up bent and twisted.

The struggles we face exert tremendous pressure on our families. Those sins and dysfunctions that we don't deal with put a heavy burden on our children. It is a constant stress on them—spiritually, emotionally, financially, socially, and physically—making it almost impossible for them to grow up healthy and strong. They will become bent or twisted because of our negative tendencies and behavior.

That's the reality we face as parents. Our actions affect more than our own lives and future; they affect the lives and future of our children for generations to come. Our problems are impacting them in ways that we probably will never imagine.

Your life was affected by those who have gone before you. And how you live will affect those who will go after you.

That's why it is so critical for us to deal with our sins and iniquities before they have a chance to revisit our families in coming generations.

The Habits We Learn

We are all imperfect people. We live in a fallen world, and sin is a reality we all deal with. We all have pain and dysfunction in our spirits to some degree unless we have dealt with it. And we all struggle to overcome the negative habits and patterns of our past. We are all victims of the lies the enemy has whispered into our spirits, and none of us have come away from our past without wounds.

God never expects us to be perfect parents, and I have no intention of placing undue guilt on those who are struggling. But it's also important that we not sweep this spiritual truth under the rug. What we do matters. It matters to God, and it matters to our children.

How we live sets the tone for our family for generations to come. It's a law of the universe, set in place by the Creator himself.

If you grew up in an angry household, chances are good that you struggle with anger issues. Have you ever heard someone say they were born with a hot temper? I honestly don't think that's possible. I don't think a temper is something you are born with. A person might be born with a propensity toward certain moods or dispositions, but a temper is something you learn. A temper is allowing yourself to strike out in anger when something doesn't go your way. And it's a learned response.

If you grew up seeing your parents impulsively lash out when they got angry, chances are good that you learned that response at home. Or you may have learned it from a friend or close relative. But I don't believe you were born with that trait. You learned it. And anything you learn can be unlearned. A temper is something that people can teach themselves to control.

Chauvinism is another learned trait. Men who grow up in a home where women are discounted or put down will likely struggle with chauvinistic tendencies. It may not be an overt quality but something they feel in their spirits. They believe that men are more capable than women, and it comes out in subtle ways when they act and speak.

Most chauvinists would never admit to their problem, because it's not always a conscious trait or belief. But others quickly pick up on it—especially their wives and children.

176

Abuse is one of the more damaging patterns of behavior that we learn. People who grow up in homes where family members are abused, either physically or emotionally, are more likely to repeat that pattern when they have families of their own.

Common sense might tell you that people who are abused by their parents would never abuse their children, simply because they've seen the harm it does. And there are cases where that is true. But statistically, children of abuse are more likely to become abusers. They learned from their parents that when you get mad, you hit. When someone makes you angry, you lash out at them verbally and/or physically. When we see our parents relating that way, we are far more likely to follow their example than we are to shun it and take a different approach.

Racism is another damaging learned behavior. Children who grow up hearing their parents slander a certain race of people are very likely to internalize and repeat those same feelings of racism when they grow older. I don't believe any child is born a racist. Children are born color-blind. Hatred based on skin color is either caught or taught at a young age.

Bigotry, pride, dishonesty, materialism, gossip, greed, immorality, negativity, sexism, sexual abuse, perfectionism, insensitivity—all these things are negative patterns of behavior that children learn from their parents. Not that we don't all have a sin nature and can do these things on our own. But when negative behaviors are modeled for children year after year, those behaviors become deeply imprinted within their hearts and minds. And these things can be passed down from one family member to another, from one generation to the next.

These are the "bends" and "twists" God is referring to when he speaks about the sin of the parents that is passed down to the children "to the third and fourth generation."

The Habits We Repeat

How many times as a child did you see your parents act a certain way or speak a certain phrase, and then say to yourself, "I'm never going to do that when I grow up"? Chances are good that once you started having kids of your own, you found yourself doing the exact thing you said you'd never do.

My dad was a good man, but he was a strict disciplinarian. He didn't put up with much nonsense from his kids. We would never imagine talking disrespectfully to him, because we knew exactly what that would get us.

My dad had this little habit when he saw us acting out. He would immediately snap his fingers at us. It was like his shot over the bow, letting us know that we were about to get it if we didn't straighten up. And his snap was loud and piercing. You could hear it from across the house. When we heard that noise, we instinctively paid attention.

Often my brothers and I would be playing in the den, wrestling on the floor, and our roughhousing would start to get out of hand. We'd begin knocking over furniture or get too loud, and suddenly we'd hear our dad snap his fingers. Immediately we'd settle down.

My dad wasn't mean, but he was serious about keeping his boys in line. And that snap was his way of letting us know we were about to push him too far. It drove me crazy, and I promised myself that I would never do that when I had a family of my own. I would simply let my kids play or calmly touch them on the shoulder and say, "You boys need to play a little quieter" before going about my business.

Then I had kids. And the first time I saw them acting up, I raised my hand and snapped my fingers at them, just like my dad used to do. I didn't even know it was loaded. It just went off without notice. I distinctly remember thinking to myself, "Where did that come from?"

And that's not the only habit I picked up from my dad. So many of the phrases I say to my kids, or the ways I relate to them, are exactly the things I learned from him when I was a kid. Many of them are things I promised myself I would never say or do.

Not all of them are harmful or damaging behaviors, but some are. And those are the ones I knew years ago I had to address.

Choosing Your Legacy

How did your parents resolve conflicts when you were young? Did they hit? Did they scream? Did they curse? Did they get angry and stop speaking for days on end? Did they emotionally or physically abuse each other?

Today, do you find yourself repeating those same patterns of behavior?

If so, it's time to unlearn the things you learned from your parents. At some point you have to stop and say to yourself, "Enough is enough!" At some point in life you have to recognize the negative patterns of relating and decide once and for all to put them behind you and change the course of your future.

How did your parents handle their finances? Were they generous givers or stingy with their money? Did they live with too much debt? Did you grow up with a spirit of poverty in your home? Or did you grow up with a spirit of blessing and provision?

Chances are you picked up a lot of financial "bends" and "twists" from your parents. If you struggle with money and never seem to have enough, you likely learned many of your negative financial habits from them.

How did your parents treat each other? Did your mother honor your father and treat him with respect, or did she put him down and treat him with condescension and contempt? And how did your father treat your mother? Did he treat her with love and tenderness, or did he ignore her needs and feelings?

What you saw at home is likely the pattern you've repeated in your own marriage. Your attitude toward your spouse is likely the same attitude you experienced from your parents as a child.

These are the questions we all need to ask ourselves. These are the things we need to assess and reevaluate in our lives, because these are the things that are putting direct pressure on the lives of our children. These are the things that are likely causing them to bend and twist as they fight to navigate their future. These are the habits and patterns of behavior that they will be struggling with in their own lives and families.

If your parents had a certain "bent," and you see the same bent in your own life, it's time to confront the problem head-on before it passes to your children's children.

There are some things out of our control. We can't control our bloodline. We can't change what was done by generations before us. We can't control those negative patterns of behavior that our parents struggled with. We can't do anything about the damaging and destructive habits we saw as children.

But we can control what our children experience. We can change the way we choose to relate to our families and our spouses. We can control what we do with our own pain and dysfunction.

We can take responsibility for the things we say and the way we act at home. We are all free to rise above our circumstances. We are free to forgive the sins of our past and move forward.

We are all free to change. And with the help of God's Spirit, we have the power to change as well.

No one has to pass on a legacy of pain. We all have the power to choose the legacy we leave behind.

_____ *Takeaway*_____

- We are all living between generations, and we all have two legacies that face us. The first is the legacy that has gone before us. The second is the legacy we will leave behind.

- When parents live in sin and disobedience to God it puts tremendous pressure on their children, making it difficult for them to grow up healthy—both spiritually and emotionally.

- The behaviors we witnessed from our parents are likely some of the same traits and habits we will model for our own children. These behaviors, both good and bad, will have a marked impact on our children's future, often for generations to come.

$-14-$

Breaking the Cycle

Childhood suffering is not a mortal wound, and it did not irrevocably shape your destiny. . . . Just as the pain, hurt, and suffering that came to you as a child were powerfully real, so is the tangible resilience of your spirit.

—*Wayne Muller*

There is a cemetery in Memphis, Texas, just on the outskirts of town. It's a quiet and peaceful place, and since a lot of my ancestors came from the area, it's where many of my relatives are buried.

One day I was visiting the cemetery with my father. We were there alone, standing in front of my great-grandmother's gravesite.

My dad had always been a quiet man who kept his thoughts and emotions to himself. He seldom talked about his past or his feelings—or much else that was going on inside his head. That used to frustrate me as a kid. I often wanted to have deep discussions with my father and get to know him better, but that wasn't his way. He was the strong, silent type. When he spoke, people listened, because they knew he didn't speak unless he had something worth saying.

Because of his quiet disposition, I never knew much about my heritage. I'd heard a lot of stories here and there about things that happened in our family, but never quite knew the details of my father's life.

My dad's family was dirt poor. And if you're from the South, you know that "dirt poor" is the worst kind of poverty. He grew up in a one-room house with nine other siblings, so he ended up sleeping outside every night. In the wintertime he moved into the barn and slept with the horses. And he was lucky to eat meat one day a week. He lived during the Depression, and his parents had very little money to their names.

In spite of their crippling poverty, my dad's parents were very giving people. I had often heard stories of the Depression and of how tough things were on his family. But even though they barely had enough to feed themselves, his mother would regularly feed other families in the area. Men would line up at their back door, and my grandmother would give them soup and bread and anything else she could scare up. She was a remarkable woman, respected by everyone who knew her.

But my father still grew up with a lot of pain, and each time I heard the stories my relatives would tell about his childhood, I found myself wondering how he ever got through it. He endured a tremendous amount of suffering and grief, yet you would never know that about him. And given what I know about his upbringing, I think he came out of it amazingly well-rounded.

I often wonder if my dad didn't talk much about his past because he was trying so hard to forget it. He didn't want to revisit his pain any more than he wanted to pass it on to his children. So he kept his thoughts inside, hoping the misery would stay there as well.

That isn't a healthy way to deal with pain, but it's the only way he knew. It's remarkable to me how little dysfunction he transferred to his kids, given the amount of sorrow and distress he suffered as a child.

That's another testament to my father's character.

Understanding My Past

That day, however, as he and I were sitting together at the cemetery, he began to open up to me. We were standing in front of his grandmother's gravesite. His grandfather's gravesite was right next to it. Many other relatives were buried nearby.

My dad began to tell me stories from his childhood, and I learned things I had never known before. I'd always known that my grandmother and her siblings had been raised in an orphanage, but I'd never been told the sad circumstances behind that story. Some of the stories he told about the things she went through as a child sent chills down my spine. She suffered an enormous amount of pain and sorrow in her life.

He also told me stories of his father and the tremendous heartache he had suffered as a child. And then he told me stories of his own childhood, of what it felt like to grow up during the Depression, of the helplessness and vulnerability he had experienced. I'd always heard that my dad had to go to work at a young age to help support his family, but I had never heard about the grueling jobs he was forced to take and the difficulties he had suffered during those years.

I had also never heard about the dreams he had to give up so he could help take care of his family.

As I sat listening to my father tell stories of our family's history—stories of poverty and war and sin, stories of death and disease and sickness—I suddenly started to see my parents in an entirely different light. I began to understand things that I had never before been able to reconcile.

When I saw the legacy of my past, I suddenly understood a lot of the struggles and pain my family had been through. It also explained a lot about my own struggles in life. Though I don't blame my parents for the pain and problems I've suffered, I do see a connection to those things in the roots of my past.

It sheds a lot of light on your life when you understand the darkness through which your family has traveled.

Changing Your Legacy

I gained a great deal of insight into my father's life that day, and the more I learned about his childhood, the more I respected the man that he had become. I don't think I realized until that moment how much pain and abuse had been passed down to my parents through the generations before them.

Early in our marriage, Karen and I were on a dangerous path of anger and emotional abuse. If God hadn't stepped in and changed our course, we likely would have passed on a great deal of pain to our children. We certainly made mistakes that affected our children, but by God's grace we were able to break the cycle of generational sin and pain before they were permanently touched by it.

With God's help, we all have the power to heal the emotional wounds in our spirits and break the negative patterns of behavior that have haunted us. We don't have to repeat the cycles of abuse and pain.

With God's help, we all have the power to change our lives and choose the legacy we leave behind.

Taking Responsibility for Your Actions

We all have negative patterns of behavior that we'd like to change. No one gets through life untouched by sin or immune to the devil's lies. That was true for your parents, and it's true for you.

When I speak I often ask two rhetorical questions. I tell people not to raise their hands, but many do anyway.

The first question I ask is, "How many of us, especially those of us who are older, spent years of our adult lives struggling to overcome the problems of our past?"

Just about every adult in the room nods in agreement. They all seem to know exactly what I'm talking about, and they can all relate.

Then I ask a second question: "How many of you would like your children and grandchildren to grow up not having to deal with those problems?"

And that's usually when the hands instinctively raise high in the air. We all want our children and their children to have a better life than we've had. But for that to happen, we have to make some hard choices and deal with the sins and iniquities in our own lives.

It's easy to blame our problems on our parents, because they almost always pass on negative patterns of behavior to us. But it's important to acknowledge that in spite of what they did or didn't do, all of the sinful patterns we develop as adults are the results of our own choices. And there comes a time when we have to take responsibility for our actions and deal with our problems like adults.

Freedom from iniquities, generational sins, and personal failures in our lives begins by taking responsibility. Most of us can look back and pinpoint the root sources of our struggles. In many cases the problems we are dealing with can be traced to our parents, or maybe a sibling, a coach, an uncle or aunt, or a trusted spiritual leader.

But the root of the problem isn't the real issue. And knowing why we act out isn't the key to freedom. Freedom comes when we take responsibility for our behavior and begin dealing with our problems head-on.

Whatever problem you are dealing with—whether it is an eating disorder, alcoholism, sexual addiction, depression, or any of the myriad issues that can stem from our parents and our past—freedom will never come through pointing fingers or transferring the blame. In fact, blame transfer only serves to make the problem worse. That is how bondage continues and even carries over to future generations.

Freedom comes when we begin to acknowledge our poor life choices and then take the necessary steps to break the cycle of sin and dysfunction. Freedom comes when we take responsibility for our actions, admit our failings, then commit to taking the needed steps toward changing our future.

The fact that you are reading this book tells me that you are willing to do that. It tells me that you want more for your children than a legacy of hurt and dysfunction. It tells me that you want to provide a better future and a better heritage. Like Karen and me, you've committed to putting an end to the painful legacy of your past and have instead committed to leaving a blessed future for the generations to come.

And the most critical step toward seeing that happen is to begin taking responsibility for your actions. Only then can God begin the healing process. Only then can God come alongside and help break the damaging cycle of sin and dysfunction that has held you hostage.

Breaking the Cycle

Just like those twisted trees in West Texas grow with a bent toward the northeast because of the prevailing southwest winds, a parent's behavior produces a prevailing influence on a child's mind, heart, and emotions. And if that influential force is filled with sin and dysfunction, it will cause them to grow up with a bent toward those same types of negative behaviors.

If you were raised in an environment of abuse or neglect or shame, you are likely struggling with those same issues in your own family. And you might be passing on those same destructive traits to your children.

Perhaps you grew up in an atmosphere of pride and judgmentalism. You regularly heard your parents disrespecting others because they were poor or uneducated, or because of their political or religious differences. And now you cringe each time you hear the same type of words coming out of your own mouth.

Or maybe you were raised in a house of fear and worry. Perhaps your mother struggled with deep bouts of depression and anxiety, and you spent much of your childhood trying to comfort her. She would lean on you for support, and you would do your best to help. And because of it, you learned to keep your own problems hidden from sight. Today you have kids of your own, and you've found yourself struggling with those same bouts of depression that haunted your mother. And all too often you've caught yourself looking to your kids for emotional support.

So how do you break the cycle?

After you've taken responsibility for your actions, you submit those areas of sin and dysfunction to the Lord and surrender your struggles to the transforming power of God's Word. You commit yourself to prayer and study, and ask God to give you the power to change.

The Bible is so much more than a book of training and teaching. It isn't just a book of religious thoughts and ideas. It is the very breath of God. Hebrews 4:12–13 tells us:

> For the word of God is alive and active. Sharper than any double-edged sword, it penetrates even to dividing soul and spirit, joints and marrow; it

judges the thoughts and attitudes of the heart. Nothing in all creation is hidden from God's sight. Everything is uncovered and laid bare before the eyes of him to whom we must give account.

Unlike any other book in the world, you don't just read the Bible; it reads you! Each time you allow God's Word into your life, it is like a two-edged sword. One edge is healing the scars and pain of your inner person—infiltrating those hurting places where no person could ever go—while the other edge is slaying the enemies that are nesting in the darkness of your hurt pocket.

Verse 13 says, "Nothing in all creation is hidden from God's sight." And that is exactly what it means. Every entity that is against us, keeping us in pain, holding us in bondage to the failures of our past and the problems of our present, is exposed by the Word of God. They cannot hide from God's sight. When we surrender our iniquities and issues to God and then find passages that apply to those areas, God's absolute and perfect truths come into our hearts and minds. They flush out pain and dysfunction like hungry hound dogs chasing a varmint. God's Word is alive and powerful and able to discern every thought and intent of our hearts.

No other book, person, expert, doctor, psychiatrist, or self-help guru can do that. And we cannot do that for ourselves. We all know that we have certain thoughts within us—some good and some bad. But the Word of God traces down the hidden, subliminal thoughts implanted long ago by the Hurt Whisperer. It shines the light of truth on them, disarms them, and renders them forever powerless. Not only that, but the Word then implants eternal truth into our hearts to guide us from that point forward.

Karen and I have experienced this many times in the course of our Christian lives, and it is a powerful dynamic. Our lives have been transformed by God's Word.

Anytime we find ourselves struggling with a particular sin or issue, we seek out a text from the Bible that speaks directly to that issue. Then we meditate on the passage, reading it over and over until it seeps into our hearts and spirits. We memorize the verses and then repeat them to ourselves as we go about our day. We immerse our struggle in the truth of God's Word, and eventually the struggle subsides.

We've discovered that God's Word will not only set you free; it will give you the power to stay free. The word *disciple* in the Bible literally means "learner." So being a disciple of Jesus means becoming a learner of God's Word. And living in freedom is the process of continually learning.

As we humbly admit our issues, submit them to God, and take them to the Word, our lives are transformed. And when we change, our family changes. Our future changes. And our children are left with a legacy of freedom and truth instead of sin and dysfunction.

And the very best news of all is this: It is never too late to start. Even if your children are grown and have families of their own, your behavior can still have a powerful effect on them and generations to come.

A New Legacy

We all understand that no one is perfect, and none of us will ever be perfect parents. God doesn't expect that of us, and neither do our children.

But being perfect is not the goal. The goal is to surrender our lives to God and continually lean on him for strength as we strive to build better lives for ourselves and our children. The goal is to give our pain and insecurities to God and let him do a miracle in our lives. To let him change us from the inside out—moment by moment, day by day, week by week. To allow God access to those dark and painful wounds that have been hiding in our spirits so that he can begin the healing process.

Our goal is to finally come out of hiding and deal with those things that have kept us in bondage to sin or addiction or offenses from our past.

Our goal is to give our pain a name so that God can remove it from our lives. Then once we've taken responsibility and surrendered to God and his Word, we set our sights on changing the future for our children. We begin looking to a new day and a brand-new legacy of hope.

Breaking the cycle of hurt is a process that only God can get us through. But we have to believe with every fiber of our being that he can—and will—get us through it.

Takeaway

- When you see the legacy of your past, it sheds a lot of insight on your family's dynamics. You begin to understand your parents' struggles when you see the pain they've gone through.

- With God's help, we all have the power to change our negative patterns of behavior and break the legacy of hurt that has plagued our family for generations.

- Changing our legacy begins by taking responsibility for our actions and submitting those areas of pain and struggle to God. Only then can he bring healing and redirect the course of our future.

—15—

A Generational Blessing

One generation plants the trees, and another gets the shade.

—*Chinese proverb*

Blessed are those who fear the LORD, who find great delight in his commands. Their children will be mighty in the land; the generation of the upright will be blessed.

—*Psalm 112:1–2*

As a young boy I played a lot of sports, and I never understood why my dad didn't come to my games. I played just about every sport I had time for, mostly baseball and football, and a lot of my friends' fathers showed up on the sidelines. But for some reason my dad never came.

It wasn't as if he didn't enjoy sports, because I knew he did. I also knew that he supported my love of playing. Anytime I needed a new glove or some shoulder pads he'd find a way to get them for me, even when times were tough. He just always seemed to be working when there was a big game.

So often I would be at bat, standing over the plate, and I could feel in my bones that I was *this close* to knocking one into the hereafter. Just before setting up I'd glance over at the bleachers to see if my dad might have sneaked in late. But he was never there.

Other times I'd make a big play during an important game or complete a critical tackle right when the team needed it, and when we got home I'd stand in the middle of the living room and tell my dad all about it. I'd say to him, "You should have been there, Daddy! It was awesome!"

Then later that night I'd lie awake in bed, trying to drift off to sleep, and I'd find myself thinking, "Yeah, Daddy, you should have been there. I really wanted you to be there."

I can't pretend that it didn't hurt, because it did. Sometimes it hurt deeply. And I always wrestled with a lot of anger and resentment because of his absence. Quite honestly, it probably added to the deep feelings of insecurity I was already struggling with during those years.

I never said anything to him about my feelings, but I always wondered why he would rather be working than watching me play. In many ways it didn't make sense to me.

Understanding My Dad's Past

Then one day, years later, I was visiting with two of my dad's sisters. They were laughing and reminiscing about the days of their youth and telling funny stories about my dad as a kid. I always loved it when my aunts told stories, because they were so fun and animated. Suddenly one of them mentioned something that reminded them of the Depression, and instantly the tone turned serious and the laughter stopped.

That's something I saw a lot during my childhood. Many families suffered a lot of pain during those years, and my family was no exception.

My aunts told me that day that my dad never had a pair of shoes until his first day of school in the first grade. He went to class barefoot that day and was laughed at by the other kids, so he ran out of the building and grabbed hold of a tree in the front of the school yard. He wrapped his arms around the tree, buried his face in the trunk, and wouldn't let go. Eventually his parents came to get him and take him home. That's when he got his first pair of shoes.

Every time someone told stories about my father's childhood I'd learn a little bit more about the devastating poverty he lived through.

And each story added another layer of understanding and sadness to my heart. I can't imagine the shame he must have felt, the humiliation of sleeping outside on a cot because there was no more room in the house, the hopelessness of wondering whether there would be food on the table when he got home, the disgrace of walking around barefoot because his parents couldn't afford shoes. I can't imagine what that must have been like.

As I sat talking with my aunts on the porch that day, my mind drifted back to all those days on the field when I'd look over at the bleachers and see the other fathers, knowing that my dad was still working at the appliance store. I thought back to all the times I resented him for not being there, and for the first time in my life I finally understood what it was that kept him away. It wasn't that he didn't care for me; it was that he did care. And he cared deeply.

I've spent a lot of my life preaching about the damaging inner vows I struggled with as a kid, but it never occurred to me until that moment that my dad likely had a few inner vows of his own. He had been deeply wounded by poverty in his life, and he was determined to see that his kids never experienced the shame and hopelessness that defined his childhood. So he vowed to himself that he would never let his kids grow up hungry. He would never allow them to be shamed and embarrassed by poverty.

All those days when I was playing with my friends on the field, my dad was working long hours at the appliance store, struggling to make ends meet, all the while thinking to himself, "Jimmy will survive me not being at his game, but that boy's never going to go without shoes!"

I suddenly felt guilty for ever allowing myself to believe that he would rather be stuck at work than watching me play. His inner vow simply wouldn't allow him to have fun when it could mean the possibility of financial failure. I thought he didn't care about me, but I suddenly realized that the only thing he didn't care about was himself.

At that moment I could literally feel all the anger and resentment I had harbored in my heart for so many years completely lift from my spirit. I saw deeper into my father's heart than I had ever seen before, and I finally understood. I finally realized what motivated him to get up so early every morning and stay at the store long after everyone else had gone home. I realized what it was that pushed him to struggle so hard.

It wasn't ambition that drove him. It was love. It was complete and unwavering selflessness. It was his determination to never allow his children to experience the soul-numbing devastation that he was forced to live with.

My father simply refused to pass on the pain and shame that had done so much damage to his own heart and spirit. And he never once complained about the sacrifices it took to keep that from happening.

In many ways, that day on the porch was a defining moment in my life. It was the day that I was finally able to forgive my father for not being there when I wanted him. It was the day that so many feelings of insecurity and offense were set free from my heart for good. It was the day that I finally was able to make peace with my past.

False Perceptions

So often the pain and insecurity we experience in life are not as deliberate or intentional as our memories project them to be. Our feelings get hurt and our fragile egos immediately start looking for people and places on which to lay the blame.

I can look back on my life and see so many times when I felt insulted or discounted by someone, and my overactive imagination would run amok with accusations. But much of the pain and insecurity I dealt with as a child was more a matter of misunderstanding than abuse.

I spent so many years of my life angry with the people who had authority over me, rebelling in school because of the way I thought I had been mistreated, acting out in class because I was so sure the teachers and principals were out to get me. But that was never the case. All I was doing was shaking my fist in the dark at some faceless bureaucrat, making myself miserable in the process.

I look back at all the times I was angry with my father for not being at my games, convinced that he was just uninterested in my life, but now I understand that it had nothing to do with indifference. He loved me deeply, and he was doing the best he could to make sure I had everything I needed.

I think back to all the days during the early years of our marriage when I was convinced that Karen was trying to control me, trying to put me down and disrespect me as a husband, but all she was doing was trying to survive my abrasive personality and stubborn attitude.

So many of the offenses I perceived were brought on by my own inability to navigate the emotions I was feeling. And most of the time Satan was right there beside me, whispering into the depths of my spirit, "No one cares about you. No one loves you. No one wants you around."

We are all deeply affected by the wounds of our past. And so much of the pain we experience is made worse by the messages the Hurt Whisperer implants within them.

The problem with that reality is that it's impossible to be the blessing we should be to those around us unless we first make peace with our past.

Making Peace with Your Past

One thing I've discovered during my years of counseling is that people often have a hard time admitting that their parents weren't perfect. They start to open up about some offense they felt as a child, and suddenly they will stop themselves and say something like, "I really can't blame my mom, because she was a wonderful mother. It was really all my fault."

It doesn't surprise me, because we never want to think poorly of the ones we love. There's something in us that recoils at the thought of sharing family secrets with a stranger. It somehow feels devious and disloyal—like we're betraying a sacred trust.

But there's nothing disloyal about admitting that your parents had problems. I had wonderful parents who loved my brothers and me deeply, but they weren't perfect. They struggled just like we all do. They didn't always make the best decisions, and sometimes they acted more out of fear than common sense. Like all of us, my parents were doing the best they could to navigate the confusion and frustration of life, and in the process they made mistakes.

And it's not a betrayal of my family's honor for me to admit that fact.

Today my kids are adults who have children of their own, and I'm certain that there are days when they lie awake at night thinking, "Dad really hurt my feelings when he said that. I wish he had been more sensitive." I shouldn't feel betrayed by that, because I'm only human. My children know how much I love them. They know I did all I could to be the best father I knew how to be for them, and that's what really matters.

If there are things that your family did right, remember those things and brag about them to your friends. But when you recognize those things that your parents did wrong, don't be afraid to acknowledge them. Admit their faults and shortcomings, and use that knowledge to keep yourself from repeating the mistakes they made.

Then forgive your parents for being human. Forgive them for the ways they hurt you. Forgive them for the times you felt ignored or slighted or disrespected. Forgive them for the days that they were too worried or distracted with their own problems to tend to your needs. Forgive them for the times they embarrassed you in front of your friends, for the moments that they leaned on you instead of letting you lean on them, for the times that they forgot to pick you up from school or didn't make it to your big recital. And forgive them for their bigger mistakes of abandonment, abuse, addiction—those things that aren't just painful but devastating.

Forgive them for all the things they said and did, as well as the things they didn't say or do. Forgiveness is essential in being set free and in emptying the hurt pockets in our hearts. Forgiveness simply means we release the judgment of a person and bring their account with us to zero. They owe us nothing, and we will do nothing to pay them back.

And true forgiveness is unconditional. It isn't based on the response we get or the remorse we sense from the one who wounded us. In many cases, the person from our past whom we need to forgive is unaware or unrepentant, and they're often unwilling to take responsibility for their actions. But that's not important. What's important is our willingness to forgive, regardless of the offense, just as we have been forgiven.

Someone once said, "Forgiveness doesn't make the other person right, it just makes you free."

Jesus said the same thing, but in a different way. "Love your enemies, do good to those who hate you, bless those who curse you, pray for those who mistreat you. . . . Do to others as you would have them do to you" (Luke 6:27–28, 31).

When we refuse to forgive, the offense becomes an invisible umbilical cord connecting us to the person who did us wrong and binding us to the pain of their offense. And this cord feeds us with bitter memories and harsh feelings. The only way to be free of the pain and resentment is to cut the cord. To sever the painful tie that binds us. To break loose of our anger and set ourselves free. To truly forgive so that we can move forward.

Often when I counsel people who are struggling with a painful past, I encourage them to write out a list of all the people in their lives whom they feel have offended them, beginning with their parents. We pray together, asking God to give them a clear memory of every person they need to forgive. Then I ask them to take the list home and pray through it one name at a time.

I encourage them to find time each day to sit down with the list and begin forgiving each person individually. I ask them to say the name aloud and speak words of forgiveness over them. Then they are to pray blessings over that person, just as Jesus commanded us to do. And they are to pray this blessing every day until it becomes a reality in their heart and spirit.

There is a supernatural healing to be found through the act of forgiveness. It is the secret to emotional and spiritual freedom. And it is the only way to truly make peace with the pain of your past.

Letting Go of Your Inner Vows

Once you've made peace with your family's past, it's time to give yourself a break as well. It's time to let go of the shame and regret and insecurity that still simmer in your spirit. It's time to turn loose of those destructive inner vows that have caused so much pain and damage to your heart.

Inner vows are always made in order to keep us from getting hurt, but once they reside in our spirits, they begin to systematically compromise us from the inside out. And we will never find true inner peace until we allow God to remove them from our hearts.

Inner vows take on so many shapes and forms that often we have a hard time recognizing them. But once they take hold, they silently guide our lives, constantly controlling the things we say and do, forever holding us hostage to fear.

A teenage girl lies in bed crying because another callous boyfriend broke her heart, and she says to herself, "I'm never going to let that happen again. I'm never going to let another person get that close."

A young boy sits in his room, his arms folded across his chest, his backside still stinging from the welts left by his father's belt, and he mutters under his breath, "I'm never going to spank my kids! I'll never treat them the way Dad treats me!"

A young girl sits sulking in the backseat of her mother's car, angry because her parents couldn't afford the shoes she really wanted, and she says to herself, "I hate being poor. I'm never going to make my kids wear hand-me-downs."

And these inner vows stay with us far longer than most of us ever imagined they could. They become the ghosts that haunt us through much of our adult lives.

I'll never be poor. I'll never make my kids work this hard. I'll never let my husband treat me like that. I'll never let my wife control me. I'll never make my kids go to church.

We make inner vows in order to help us process the pain we're going through, but all they ever do is bring greater pain and distress.

I once had a friend who used to hoard soft drinks in a cabinet in his house. Every time I would visit he'd open the cabinet door and offer me a drink. He had every kind of soft drink you could imagine. And he wasn't happy unless you let him fix you a cold glass of Pepsi or Coke or Sprite, or whatever you wanted. Then when your glass was half empty he'd jump up to refill it.

I remember thinking he was the most hospitable man on the planet, until I realized it was more of an obsession with him than a desire to be cordial. His wife once joked about what it was like to go shopping with him. They would be making their way down the aisles of the grocery store, and within minutes he'd have the cart filled with soft drinks. She would say to him, "Don't you think we have enough?" and he would immediately snap back at her.

"Don't tell me I can't buy soft drinks," he would say. "I'll get as many as I want!"

One day he confided in me that his mother never allowed him to have carbonated beverages as a child. All of his friends got to have soft drinks, but he had to drink water or juice. So he said to himself, "I'm never going to deny my kids like that. They'll get to have all the soft drinks they want."

What began as a seemingly harmless inner vow grew into a full-fledged obsession. And it quickly became a serious point of friction in his marriage.

Inner vows always damage our relationships. And they make it impossible to get truly close to God in the area of the vow. At its core an inner vow is a decision of the heart to take control of our lives instead of leaning on God; and when we stop trusting God, the relationship becomes nonexistent in that area.

Inner vows keep us bound to the past. And it's impossible to look ahead toward a bright and blessed future when our hearts are still tied to pain that should have long since been erased.

Before you can move forward, you have to first turn loose of your inner vows. Until you do, they will never turn loose of you.

There is a quick and easy way to break an inner vow. And it is powerful enough to heal your heart and change your future. Just begin by confessing your inner vow to the Lord, and then lift up this simple prayer:

> Lord, I now realize that it was wrong for me to make such a damaging inner vow. When I did that, I became the lord of that area instead of surrendering that part of my life to you. I now break the inner vow and renounce it. I turn this area of my life over to you and declare that you are Lord. Forgive me, and give me the power to change as I move forward trusting in you.

Give your inner vows to God, and I promise he will do a miracle in your heart and spirit.

Planning for a Blessed Future

As a person with a strong type A personality, I learned early the importance of setting goals—both long- and short-term—and then putting together a plan of action in order to carry them out. You tackle your goals one step at a time, one small goal after another. Then before you know it, you've accomplished what you set out to do.

I've been able to achieve a lot of the goals I set for myself, only to learn later that many of them weren't really worth setting in the first place. The ones that were selfish goals, based more on my need to prove myself than a desire to help others, never quite satisfied in the way I had hoped. I've chased a lot of brass rings in life, only to find that brass is a pretty common commodity.

The only goals that mean anything to me today are the ones God was able to accomplish through me. The only achievements that make my heart sing are the ones I never would have thought to set for myself. Those things that God has done through my life will last long after I'm gone. They are the goals that will have an eternal impact because they are God's dreams, not mine.

My goals were fleeting. God's goals are always infinite and meaningful.

And today, at this stage in my life, I'm intimately aware of the fact that God has one big goal left that he wants me to accomplish before I'm gone. I'm not that old, so I'm sure he has plenty more for me to do, but there's one looming dream hanging over my head that I know God put there. And it weighs on my heart every day of my life.

God wants me to leave an inheritance of blessing for my children, and their children, and every generation thereafter. God has a deep desire to bless my descendants through my legacy. God's greatest goal for my life is that long after I'm gone, my life will still be giving him glory.

And he has the same goal for you.

God's greatest desire for every follower is that we pass on the torch of our faith to those who will come after us. He wants us to live in such a way that the blessings we leave behind will ring well into eternity and be felt by all those who travel in our wake. He wants to bring eternal honor and blessing to our descendants, and he wants to do that for countless generations to come.

God wants to do so much more than bless our lives; he wants to bless the *bloodline* of our lives. And he desires for us to partner with him in this miraculous covenantal promise of blessing.

A Covenantal Promise

A few chapters ago we discussed the damage that sin brings into our lives and the devastation it brings to the legacy we leave behind. We spent time examining God's dire warning to the people of Israel in the book of Deuteronomy.

> I, the LORD your God, am a jealous God, punishing the children for the sin of the parents to the third and fourth generation of those who hate me . . . (5:9)

Sin does so much more than keep us from building a relationship with God; it brings wickedness and dysfunction into the lives of our families, and can even revisit that pain on the lives of our descendants.

But there's another part to God's message to Israel that we haven't yet discussed. Anytime God gives a message of warning and wrath in Scripture, he follows it with a message of hope and restoration. And this passage is no exception.

> . . . but showing love to a thousand generations of those who love me and keep my commandments. (5:10)

A life of sin and disobedience can bring pain into our family to the "third and fourth generation," and that's far too long to give us any comfort. I don't want my children to suffer even a minute for the things I've done, and I know you don't either.

But God's promise of blessing to those who keep his commandments is a staggering pledge of compassion. He promises blessing to *a thousand generations*! And I'm not one who thinks this is just a figure of speech. When God says a thousand generations, I think that's exactly what he means. God's covenantal promise is a lasting and eternal one.

His blessings will ring into the future far beyond what you and I are capable of imagining.

A Legacy of Blessing

The thought that my small, seemingly insignificant acts of faith and obedience can have that kind of spiritual impact on my descendants— even those who might be born thousands of years from now—is a mind-boggling concept for me to grasp. I'm not sure I'm smart enough to imagine what my great-grandkids will be like, much less those descendants a thousand generations in the future.

But I can imagine my life having an impact on the lives of my precious twin granddaughters, Elle and Abby. Today they are only eleven years old, but if I close my eyes I can visualize what they might be like when they're my age. I imagine they'll be just as beautiful as their grandmother is today. And I think they'll have her sweet spirit and kind disposition as well.

They'll likely have grandkids of their own by then. And their grandkids will be as precious and pretty as our grandkids are. Maybe they'll be twins too.

I wonder if Elle and Abby will remember all the times Karen and I babysat them while their parents went out for dinner. I wonder if they'll remember all the long walks we took around the block. The trips to the zoo, when I held them on my shoulders so they could see the tigers better and so the monkeys wouldn't get them. The many times they came to see us for the holidays and we all laughed around the table long after the food was gone. The nights I wrestled with them in the living room, then bounced them on my knee until they got tired. The stories I read to them just before their mother took them off to tuck them into bed.

I wonder if they'll have a faded photo of Karen and me on the mantel, telling their friends stories about "Lollie and Pappy Evans," their mom's parents who grew up in Texas and even had their own television show once.

I wonder if they'll have an old, worn-out copy of this book on their bookshelf.

Most of these things I can only wonder about, but there's one thing I can know for certain. I know that my life—the things I choose to do today, the decisions I make hour by precious hour—will have a marked difference on the quality of my granddaughters' lives.

I know that my faith will have an impact on their faith. I know that my choices will impact their choices. I know that my decision to trust God in every circumstance will strengthen their resolve to trust God as well, long after I've gone to be with the Lord in eternity.

I don't ever want to take the promise of God's blessing for granted. And I want my precious granddaughters, along with every generation beyond them, to be the spiritual beneficiaries of that divine blessing.

I hope and pray that for your children as well.

Takeaway

- We are all deeply affected by the pain of our past. But much of the pain we've experienced is not as deliberate or intentional as we might have imagined. For most of us, our parents were doing the best they could. Like all of us, they had struggles of their own to deal with.

- Healing begins when we decide to make peace with our past and forgive our parents for the offenses we have held against them, as well as for the things they did that left us wounded—whether deliberate or unintentional.

- Once we've made peace with our past, it's time to make peace with ourselves. And this begins by turning loose of the damaging inner vows that have held us hostage to pain.

- God's desire for believers is that we leave behind a legacy of blessing. To those who keep his commandments, he has promised to bless our children for a thousand generations. And that promise is available for each and every one of us.

Eight-Week Study Guide

For Individuals or Small Groups

Allowing God to heal unresolved pain and dysfunction is a process. It takes intentional time and effort to work through years of deep-seated, hidden wounds from the past. And that journey is much lighter and easier when you don't try to go it alone.

The following eight-week study guide is designed to help facilitate your road to healing and walk you through the process. Whether you are working through this study alone or in a small group setting, the questions are intended to help you gain insight and understanding of your pain as you seek God for inner healing. I encourage you to take your time and work through this study slowly and deliberately, one question at a time, and not rush through the process. Pray and meditate on your answers, letting each thought sink in before moving forward.

I believe the best approach to doing this is in a small group setting. If you're presently involved in a small group, perhaps you can suggest this guide for a future resource. And if you're not in a small group, this might be a good opportunity to start one. Whatever you decide, I hope you'll take advantage of this resource.

Here's how the study guide works: Each week's lesson walks you through two chapters of the book, except for the final week, which covers the final chapter. You'll get more out of this study if you take time to read each chapter and then answer the questions before your next meeting. This will give you time to reflect on your answers in private and process your thoughts before coming together with the group.

Each lesson also ends with an applicable Scripture for meditation. I encourage you to take time each week to reflect on this passage and pray that God would reveal how it applies to your life and what divine truth he would reveal to you through his Word.

Remember that only God can bring true healing and restoration. But in order for him to do that, we have to first seek his help and lean on him as he begins the process. My prayer is that God will use this book, and this study guide, to help you do just that.

Week 1

Chapter 1—Pictures of Pain

1. Many of us fill our homes with photographs of pleasant times and happy memories. Describe some of the photographs that decorate the walls and shelves of your home. What pleasant memories come to mind as you look at these photos?

2. In what ways have these pleasant memories shaped your thoughts and guided your future?

3. God often uses pleasant memories to guide us toward our purpose and help us become the people he longs for us to be. How have you found this to be true in your life? In what ways have your good memories had an eternal impact on your life?

4. Tragic and bad memories also have a way of silently guiding our lives and shaping our future. Can you think of some devastating moments and events that have had a marked impact on your life? If you're comfortable doing so, share these memories with the group.

5. I'm convinced that every story of addiction and dysfunction is somehow rooted in pain. Every person I counsel, without exception, is dealing with some form of deep-seated, unresolved pain from their past. What would you say are some unprocessed and unresolved issues you still struggle with from your past?

6. I describe the "hurt pocket" as that place where unresolved pain and wounds go to hide and fester. And the more pain that builds inside of us, the more it compromises our mental, emotional, and spiritual health. If you had to describe the contents of your hurt pocket at this moment, how would you put it into words? What are some of the unresolved pain issues that remain hidden deep inside your heart and spirit?

7. How have you attempted to give your pain to God in the past? In what ways have you been able to do that? In what ways have your efforts to find healing been unfruitful?

8. Why is it important to journey with others as we learn to let God heal our unprocessed pain, instead of trying to go it alone?

9. Galatians 6:2 tells us, "Bear one another's burdens, and so fulfill the law of Christ" (NKJV). Part of the healing process involves sharing our pain and receiving prayer support from others. Continue to think about what you would be willing to share with the group concerning pain in your life. Pray for courage to share your pain with others and for a gentle heart of wisdom as you hear the pain and concerns of others.

Chapter 2—Defining Moments

1. As a child, I was deeply hurt and confused when I was prevented from attending school with my friends. We all want to belong, to feel that we are a part of our loved ones' lives and not left out. Can you share a similar story from your past? Maybe a time when you were left feeling abandoned or marginalized by others?

2. What feelings rise to the surface as you recall these experiences?

3. In what ways are you still struggling with feelings of insecurity and doubt because of things that were said or done to you in the past?

4. We can all look back on our lives and pinpoint a handful of life-defining, negative moments—specific events or

circumstances that caught us off-guard and left us feeling confused and angry. What are some specific, life-defining events or circumstances like this from your childhood that you'd be willing to share with others?

5. In what ways do these feelings still haunt you, even as an adult?

6. If you had to describe one deep-seated feeling or insecurity from childhood that you struggle with today—something that others might be surprised to learn about you—what would you say?

7. In what ways are these damaging inner feelings affecting your daily life? How do they affect your marriage? Your relationships? Your career decisions?

8. If you haven't done so yet, begin keeping a daily journal of your prayers, struggles, and victories. You will be amazed and encouraged to see God's guiding and healing grace in your life.

Scripture Meditation

I have set before you life and death, blessings and curses. Now choose life, so that you and your children may live and that you may love the LORD *your God, listen to his voice, and hold fast to him. (Deut. 30:19–20)*

Week 2

Chapter 3—Inner Vows

1. Why is inner pain more damaging and destructive than outer pain?

2. As a young man, I dealt with the pain of my past by acting out in rebellion and anger, and I have many regrets because of my unhealthy reaction. What regrets do you have today because of the way you handled the painful moments of your childhood? How would you do things differently if you had a chance to live through those years again?

3. What are some damaging inner vows you've made during painful times?

4. How have these inner vows affected your life in negative ways? How have they affected the lives of those close to you?

5. In this chapter, we discuss three major problems with inner vows. What are these three problems?

6. How have your inner vows caused you to act out in sinful ways? How have they caused you to overreact? How have they become a guiding force in your life?

7. In what ways have inner vows damaged your relationships with your spouse? Your children? Your close friends and family members?

8. Inner vows make it impossible for us to build a deep and meaningful relationship with God. Discuss why this is true. In what ways have you allowed inner vows to damage your relationship with God?

Chapter 4—When Hurt Hides

1. Are there any wounds in the hurt pocket of your heart that you've been hoping would heal on their own in time? Have you experienced healing in those areas, or has time only made the pain worse?

2. In this chapter, I identify three unhealthy ways that many of us deal with pain: we medicate, we motivate, or we meditate. Discuss these three methods. How have you experienced this to be true—both in your own life and in the lives of those close to you?

3. "Medicators" deal with pain through an unhealthy dependence on food, drugs, alcohol, sex, or some other form of emotional medication. Discuss some other ways we medicate our pain. How have you experienced this dynamic in your own life?

4. "Motivators" deal with pain through unhealthy ambition and achievement. Have you ever found this to be true in your life? Discuss some damaging ways that unhealthy motivators are driven to act out in order to conceal the pain in their hearts.

5. "Meditators" tend to deal with pain by fixating on their problems. They become self-obsessed and often overthink everything that happens to them. What are some other characteristics of unhealthy meditators? Why is this such a damaging way to deal with pain?

6. What effects do negativity, cynicism, and unforgiveness have on our lives?

7. Jesus said, "Blessed are those who mourn, for they will be comforted" (Matt. 5:4). In your own words, describe what

Jesus was saying in this passage. Is mourning a blessing? If not, what about pain and mourning can bring blessing into our lives?

8. The wounds we try to bury give the devil an unrestricted foothold into our hearts and lives. Tell of a time when you found yourself battling Satan because of buried wounds.

Scripture Meditation

I will give you a new heart and put a new spirit in you; I will remove from you your heart of stone and give you a heart of flesh. (Ezek. 36:26)

Week 3

Chapter 5—The Message in the Pain

1. Unprocessed pain is a dangerous force, but pain in itself is not the real culprit. The true enemy is the message in the pain. What are some examples of damaging messages we receive in the midst of pain?

2. Why does Satan speak to us during times of pain? What is it about pain that causes us to be open and vulnerable to his whispered lies?

3. God also speaks to us in the midst of pain. What are some messages that God often gives us during times of pain and tragedy?

4. If God speaks to us through pain and Satan also speaks through pain, how can we tell the difference?

5. Have you ever heard the voice of God come to you in the form of a "gentle whisper"? Describe that experience.

6. Tell of a time when God used tragedy to draw you nearer to himself or to increase your faith. How did you respond?

7. What are some specific things we can do to silence Satan's lies?

Chapter 6—Whispers of the Enemy

1. Satan often causes doubt by getting us to question God. In the garden, he asked Eve, "Did God really say, 'You must not eat from any tree in the garden?'" (Gen. 3:1). What are some ways the enemy uses that same tactic today?

2. Satan's greatest strength is his subtlety. What are some ways he attempts to stay "under the radar" when trying to get us to question God?

3. We act and react according to what we feel our identity is. Why is it so important to hold on to our identity in Christ? How do we do this?

4. What lessons can we learn from God's conversation with Adam and Eve after their fall?

5. We all know the feeling of wanting to hide after sinning, but just as God covered Adam and Eve with the skins of an innocent animal, he covers us with the blood of his sinless Son. What does 1 John 1:7 say about this?

6. Why is it so important to keep short accounts and to "not let the sun go down while you are still angry" (Eph. 4:26)?

7. What does festering anger allow the devil to do?

8. Marital discord is often the result of letting Satan interpret the words and events of a couple's life. How can we keep this from happening in our own marriages? In our relationships with others?

9. Adam and Eve didn't listen to the voice of God, and they paid a heavy price for their sin. In what ways are you and I often guilty of the same thing? What are some concrete ways we can keep the devil's thoughts from becoming our thoughts?

Scripture Meditation

Be alert and of sober mind. Your enemy the devil prowls around like a roaring lion looking for someone to devour. (1 Pet. 5:8)

My sheep listen to my voice; I know them, and they follow me. (John 10:27)

Week 4

Chapter 7—Clothed in Shame

1. Did any early childhood experiences make you feel that you were a burden, less than worthy, or not deserving of blessings? Share the experience, and then discuss what it was about this event that caused you to doubt your self-worth.

2. How do we as parents unwittingly pass these feelings and attitudes on to our own children?

3. How can we break the cycles of shame and unworthiness? Read Psalm 149:4 and discuss what God says about us.

4. Read Psalm 45, with particular emphasis on verses 10–11. What does this passage tell us about God's feelings toward us? How should this truth change the way we see ourselves?

5. Do you struggle with a spirit of poverty, a lack of trust, unforgiveness, failure, or any other damaging and unhealthy mind-sets? How do these issues manifest themselves in your day-to-day life?

6. Hebrews 4:16 tells us: "Let us then with confidence draw near to the throne of grace, that we may receive mercy and find grace to help in time of need" (ESV). What does this mean in real terms for our lives?

7. Why do you think that shame is such a powerful weapon of Satan?

8. What does it take to begin truly seeing ourselves "through new eyes"? Do you feel like you are a burden to God? How can you begin seeing yourself as a blessing to him instead?

9. Ponder this sentence toward the end of this chapter: "It's amazing to me that a God who's never broken a promise could be so doubted, while a devil who's never kept a promise could be so trusted." How will you go about showing God your trust this week?

Chapter 8—Thoughts Held Captive

1. Ephesians 6:12 says, "For our struggle is not against flesh and blood, but against the rulers, against the authorities, against the powers of this dark world and against the spiritual forces of evil in the heavenly realms." How does this contradict the way we often view those who cross us? How should it impact our prayer life?

2. When faced with hardship or tragedy, do we most often react with faith or with fear? Do we praise God or blame him?

3. In this chapter we tell the stories of Ryan and Rebecca, two people with similar experiences but completely different reactions. How did these two stories affect you when you read them? When faced with tragedy, do you think you would react like Ryan? Or would you relate more to Rebecca?

4. Is there a concrete way that you have taken "every thought captive, to make it obedient to Christ"? Share your struggles and results.

5. Philippians 4:6–7 tells us, "Do not be anxious about anything, but in every situation, by prayer and petition, with thanksgiving, present your requests to God. And the peace of God, which transcends all understanding, will guard your hearts and your minds in Christ Jesus." What is our job according to this passage? What is God's job, and what is his promise to us?

6. In this chapter, I discuss three simple steps to neutralizing the enemy's voice in our spirits and overcoming negative thoughts. What are these three steps? Discuss how we can use these three steps in practical ways when fear and doubt come our way.

7. Read 1 Corinthians 2:16. In practical terms, what does it mean to have the "mind of Christ"?

8. What sorts of things tempt you to react in anger? What is at the root of these things? How can you overcome in these areas?

Scripture Meditation

He who did not spare his own Son, but gave him up for us all—how will he not also, along with him, graciously give us all things? Who will bring any charge against those whom God has chosen? It is God who justifies. Who then is the one who condemns? No one. (Rom. 8:32–34)

We demolish arguments and every pretension that sets itself up against the knowledge of God, and we take captive every thought to make it obedient to Christ. (2 Cor. 10:5)

Week 5

Chapter 9—Come Out of Hiding

1. Why is it so difficult to "come out of hiding" and confess our sins and weaknesses to others?

2. How can we overcome the fear of being transparent with others?

3. What happens when we are willing to confess?

4. Can you think of a watershed moment when an issue or relationship in your life reached a turning point? How difficult or easy was it to walk through this?

5. In your heart of hearts, are you okay with being vulnerable? If not, what is holding you back, and what can you do about it?

6. Who is the most transparent and open person you can think of? What do you admire most about this trait in them?

7. Tell of a specific time when you were able to open up to another person. What effect did it have on you? Was it a freeing or a negative experience? Discuss the reasons for that.

8. James 5:16 says, "Therefore confess your sins to each other and pray for each other so that you may be healed." This is a direct command, and yet what conditions do we often put on it?

9. Why is it so difficult to open up to a trusted friend or counselor? Discuss the fears as well as the benefits of overcoming our unwillingness to do so.

Chapter 10—Do You Want to Be Well?

1. We began the chapter with a story about a woman who allowed "crazy" to become her defining identity. Has there been a time in your life when you habitually defaulted to dysfunction? What were the effects?

2. What are the attractions or seeming "benefits" of dysfunction?

3. What mind-set is needed in order for a person to get well?

4. If you need healing for a particular issue, what is the necessary action you must take in order to partner with God in the process?

5. Discuss the faith and humility of those whom Jesus healed. They had to answer questions honestly, and sometimes the situation might have been a bit embarrassing. How far are you willing to go in order to be healed?

6. God wants to bring divine healing into our lives, but first he expects us to take responsibility for our actions. Are there any areas where you are shirking responsibility or blaming others for your situation?

7. Healing also demands a change in lifestyle on our part. What daily habits might you need to change in order to see a permanent change in your circumstances?

8. Philippians 2:13 says, "For it is God who works in you to will and to act in order to fulfill his good purpose." What do you feel that his purpose is for you? Is there anything standing in the way of that purpose being fulfilled?

9. Come alongside God's Word and his will for you today by asking for healing and for his purpose to be fulfilled in you. Discuss some specific things you can do to allow God to turn your pain into a testimony of his faithfulness.

Scripture Meditation

If we confess our sins, he is faithful and just and will forgive us our sins and purify us from all unrighteousness. (1 John 1:9)

But if we walk in the light, as he is in the light, we have fellowship with one another, and the blood of Jesus, his Son, purifies us from all sin. (1 John 1:7)

Week 6

Chapter 11—Lord of the Brokenhearted

1. We've all felt the sting of hopelessness and despair. Discuss some events in your life that left you feeling brokenhearted. In what ways were you able to lean on God for help?

2. Why does Satan attack at the point of our greatest gifting? Discuss some ways that you've experienced this truth firsthand.

3. Have you ever been discouraged from using your gifts and strengths to their fullest potential? How did you respond?

4. In Isaiah 61, we read that God wants to bind up the brokenhearted, proclaim freedom for captives, release prisoners from darkness, and proclaim the Lord's favor—among many other blessings. In what ways have you allowed a broken heart to keep you in bondage?

5. How can we practically apply the truths of Isaiah 61:1–3 and receive beauty instead of ashes, joy instead of mourning, and a lifestyle of praise instead of despair?

6. Read Psalm 34:17–18. What does this passage tell us about how God responds to brokenness and humility?

7. Tell of a time when you were crushed in spirit and felt the Lord's closeness in the midst of the pain.

8. In what ways has God used the pain of your past to draw you into a deeper and closer relationship with him?

9. How can you allow God to use your failures and brokenness to be an encouraging witness to others?

Chapter 12—Beauty for Ashes

1. Talk about a recent event that made you ask God, "Why?" How close to this event were you? How did it affect you?

2. Why does God allow tragedies to occur when he is able to prevent them? What is he trying to accomplish?

3. Hebrews 12:7 says, "Endure hardship as discipline; God is treating you as his children." While not pleasant, how can this truth give us comfort in the midst of hardship and pain?

4. Hebrews 12:11 goes on to say, "No discipline seems pleasant at the time, but painful. Later on, however, it produces a harvest of righteousness and peace for those who have been trained by it." How have you reaped a harvest of righteousness and peace after a season of hardship or discipline?

5. Would you describe your relationship with God as a struggle? What does that mean to you? Why is struggle with God such an integral part of the Christian experience?

6. Read Romans 5:3–5. What does the Bible tell us about the purpose behind suffering? What is God's ultimate goal in allowing us to go through hard times?

7. According to this passage of Scripture, what are some godly fruits produced in the midst of suffering?

8. After his resurrection, Jesus's scars remained as a testimony of his love and faithfulness. How can your scars be a part of your testimony?

9. What in your life have you considered to be lost to the ashes? Do you believe that God is able to bring beauty from it?

Scripture Meditation

My flesh and my heart may fail, but God is the strength of my heart and my portion forever. (Ps. 73:26)

Then young women will dance and be glad, young men and old as well. I will turn their mourning into gladness; I will give them comfort and joy instead of sorrow. (Jer. 31:13)

Week 7

Chapter 13—A Legacy of Pain

1. A person's legacy is a powerful and lasting thing. What do you hope people will say about you at your funeral?

2. When you think of someone with a righteous legacy, whose name comes to mind, and why?

3. Read the story of Hezekiah's death in 2 Kings 20:12–20. What did Hezekiah do during his last days to make God angry? What was God's response to Hezekiah's sin? Why did this particular sin make God so angry?

4. Hezekiah had a son named Manasseh. What was his legacy as king of Judah?

5. Manasseh actually repented toward the end of his life, but the people continued in sin despite his directives. Why is it a fallacy to think that we can do what we like as long as we repent?

6. In this chapter we discuss a number of generational sins, such as bigotry, pride, dishonesty, materialism, gossip, greed, and immorality. Which of these sins jump out at you as being problems in your family's bloodline?

7. Talk about instances where a generational sin has been broken in your family. When and how was this pattern of sin broken?

8. Have you ever found yourself repeating words or actions from a parent and wondering how it happened? Give an example.

9. What will you do to actively change a generational sin or "bent" that you don't want passed down to your children or grandchildren?

Chapter 14—Breaking the Cycle

1. When you think about your parents and grandparents, and their family circumstances as they grew up, what thoughts and feelings come to mind? What kind of legacy did they leave behind? For instance, did they leave a legacy of pain? Poverty? Anger? Abuse? Godliness? Stewardship? Love and affirmation?

2. Was there a turning point in your ancestry in which things changed markedly for the good or the bad? What was the reason for this change?

3. In your present family life, what are some specific things you've done to change a damaging family legacy? Are there some other things you'd like to change?

4. With God's help, we all have the power to change our lives and choose the legacy we leave behind. If you want to change the direction of your legacy, or improve what is already a positive one, what steps can you take today to begin this process?

5. All of the sinful patterns we develop as adults are the results of our own choices. Have you accepted and admitted this to yourself and taken full responsibility for your actions? In what ways are you still blaming your parents or other circumstances from your past?

6. Hebrews 4:12–13 tells us, "For the word of God is alive and active. Sharper than any double-edged sword, it penetrates even to dividing soul and spirit, joints and marrow; it judges the thoughts and attitudes of the heart. . . . Everything is

uncovered and laid bare before the eyes of him to whom we must give account." God's Word has a way of exposing even the most hidden sins and offenses. If you're comfortable doing so, share with the group some of the hidden iniquities that you feel God is wanting to expel from your heart and life.

7. John 8:32 says, "Then you will know the truth, and the truth will set you free." How can this knowledge set you on a permanent path toward healing and freedom?

8. Christ's legacy is one of forgiveness, salvation, and the promise of reigning with him in eternity. How should the knowledge of this truth affect our lives in the future? Pray that God will make this truth a reality in your life throughout the coming week.

Scripture Meditation

Therefore, there is now no condemnation for those who are in Christ Jesus, because through Christ Jesus the law of the Spirit who gives life has set you free from the law of sin and death. (Rom. 8:1–2)

Week 8

Chapter 15—A Generational Blessing

1. Are there some hurtful experiences you had as a child that you'd be willing to share—maybe some things your parents did or said that caused you pain?

2. In what ways do you still feel hurt by this experience?

3. Have you since discovered some truths about your parents' past that explained their actions? Why do you think their past caused them to act out in damaging ways?

4. Have you ever taken time to forgive your parents for the things they said or did that caused you harm? Would you be willing to do that today?

5. Many of us tend to be overly sensitive when it comes to pain, and often we feel slighted or insulted, even when the offense was unintentional. Can you think of a time when you may have overreacted to an offense, either from your parents or another person? What do you think caused you to overreact?

6. Why is it important to honestly acknowledge both the right and the wrong things that happened in your family's past?

7. How can we admit what mistakes our parents made while still obeying the biblical command to honor them? Is it dishonoring to our parents' legacy to admit that they had faults and failings, just as we all do? Discuss why or why not.

8. Forgiveness simply means we release the judgment of a person and bring their account with us to zero. Why is forgiveness so important, both for our earthly lives and for eternity?

9. Forgiveness doesn't make the other person right, it just makes you free. Tell of a time when you forgave someone for a serious offense. What impact did forgiveness have on your life?

10. How does an inner vow come between us, God, and others? What does an inner vow say to God?

11. What are some inner vows that you have made, or have been tempted to make, because of your past? What effect have these vows had on your life and the lives of your loved ones?

12. What is the difference between our goals and God's goals for us, both now and eternally? How can we tell the difference?

13. What is the legacy that you want to leave for your children, grandchildren, and all who come after you? What do you most hope your descendants will think about your life a hundred years from now?

14. Spend some time in prayer and reflection as you ask God to bring blessing and honor to your children, grandchildren, and all future generations to come.

Scripture Meditation

But from everlasting to everlasting the LORD's love is with those who fear him, and his righteousness with their children's children—with those who keep his covenant and remember to obey his precepts. (Ps. 103:17–18)

Jimmy Evans is founder and CEO of MarriageToday, a ministry based in Dallas, Texas, that is devoted to helping couples build strong and fulfilling marriages and families. Jimmy and his wife, Karen, are passionate about marriage. Together they cohost *MarriageToday with Jimmy and Karen*, a nationally syndicated television program broadcast weekly into over one hundred million homes in America and more than two hundred countries worldwide.

Jimmy has served as the senior leader of Trinity Fellowship Church in Amarillo, Texas, for the past thirty years. During his years of leadership, Trinity has grown from nine hundred to over ten thousand members. He also serves as an apostolic elder of Gateway Church in Southlake, Texas; is an overseer of New Life Church in Colorado Springs, Colorado; and presides over the Trinity Fellowship Association of Churches, which oversees churches in five states.

Jimmy has authored more than ten books, among which are his popular works *Lifelong Love Affair*, *Marriage on the Rock*, *Freedom from Your Past*, *7 Secrets of Successful Families*, and *Ten Steps Toward Christ*.

Jimmy and Karen have been married thirty-nine years and have two married children and four grandchildren.

Frank Martin is the author or co-author of nineteen books, including *Furious Pursuit* and *Embracing Eternity* (co-authored with Tim LaHaye and Jerry Jenkins). He is a frequent collaborator, having written books with numerous notables, including Nicky Cruz, Bill McCartney, Dr. O. S. Hawkins, and Wally Armstrong. He was also a contributing writer for the recently released *New NIV Men's Devotional Bible*.

Frank served eighteen years as a family commentary writer for Dr. James Dobson and Focus on the Family. He has been published in numerous magazines, including *Discipleship Journal*, *Marriage Partnership*, *Image*, *UpReach*, *Today's Child*, and *Pray!*

Frank and his wife, Ruthie, have been married for twenty-seven years. They currently reside in Colorado Springs, Colorado, with their two children, David and Kandilyn. For a more extensive bio, visit Frank's website at www.frankmmartin.com.

Also Available from
JIMMY EVANS

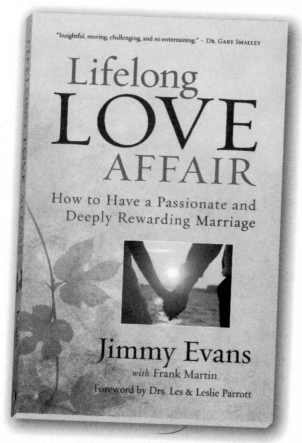

"Jimmy Evans has a way of combining Scripture with honest stories about his own marriage to show that no relationship is beyond God's help. *Lifelong Love Affair* is insightful, moving, challenging, and so entertaining. This book is full of wisdom."

—DR. GARY SMALLEY, author of *The DNA of Relationships* and *I Promise*

BakerBooks
Relevant. Intelligent. Engaging.

Available wherever books and ebooks are sold.
 ReadBakerBooks • @ReadBakerBooks

Connect with

BakerBooks
Relevant. Intelligent. Engaging.

Sign up for announcements about
new and upcoming titles at

www.bakerbooks.com/signup

 ReadBakerBooks

 ReadBakerBooks

Sample Our Newest Releases!

Videos

Book
Samples